adolescence isn't terminal

adolescence
isn't
terminal

DR. KEVIN LEMAN

Tyndale House Publishers, Inc.
Wheaton, Illinois

Visit Tyndale's exciting Web site at www.tyndale.com

Adolescence Isn't Terminal

Designed by Kelly Bennema

Edited by Lynn Vanderzalm

Some of the details and names used in the illustrations for this book have been changed to protect the privacy of people who have shared their stories with the author.

Library of Congress Cataloging-in-Publication Data

Leman, Kevin.
  Adolescence isn't terminal (it just feels like it!) / Kevin Leman.
    p. cm.
  ISBN 0-8423-5288-0 (alk. paper)
  1. Parent and teenager. 2. Parenting. I. Title.
HQ799.15 .L46 2001
649'.125—dc21   2001002238

Printed in the United States of America

06 05 04 03 02
8   7   6   5   4   3   2   1

*This book is affectionately dedicated to my
fourth-born, fourteen-year-old daughter,
Hannah Elizabeth Leman*

*Hannah love, how proud Mom and I are to be your parents. You're
fast approaching womanhood, and we both marvel at the many great
choices you have already made in life. You have nice friends and a
positive attitude about life, and most important, you are a giver, not
a taker. What did we ever do to get a daughter like you? You truly are
a gift from God. Always strive for excellence in everything you do,
and don't ever settle for less.*

May God richly bless you, Hannah. You are loved.

Your daddy—and your mom too!

contents

1

What Planet Am I On?

"CAN I COME WITH you, Daddy? Can I? I could help out at the book table."

Hannah, then thirteen years old, looked at me with those adorable, pleading eyes. How could I say no? But inwardly I smiled to myself, fully aware of what I was speaking about at the conference Hannah was asking to attend with me—information that Hannah lacked.

"Sure, honey, I'd love to have you come along," I said.

Instantly Hannah got suspicious. "What are you talking about tonight?"

"Adolescence," I said.

"Oh no," Hannah said. "Please, Daddy, please, please, *please* don't mention me. Don't say *anything* about me."

Suddenly my daughter started laughing. She hit herself on the forehead with the palm of her hand and said, "Oh no! I just gave you material for tonight, didn't I?"

Indeed she had!

At thirteen, Hannah was just breaking into that rollicking, fun, treacherous, frustrating, meaningful, and wonderful time we call adolescence. It's a contradictory period, when young teens want to be the center of the world at the same time that they don't want any attention drawn to them! They want to be perfect in all they do and in how they look, yet they also desperately desire to be just like everyone else in their peer group.

The only thing more difficult than being an adolescent is trying to parent one. I know. My wife, Sande, and I have walked three children through this process, are taking our fourth—Hannah—through it even as I write, and are getting ready for child number five—Lauren—to join what I affectionately refer to as "the hormone group."

When our kids hit that magical moment of adolescence, most of the parenting rules that helped us for the first decade of their lives become outdated. Everything changes, even as our kids change. We need to adapt, adjust, and grow in the way we relate to our kids if we want to maintain a meaningful, healthy, and strong relationship during this admittedly turbulent time.

Perhaps it would surprise you to know Sande would agree with me that our favorite stage in parenting our kids has been their time in adolescence. Though this season can be difficult, it can also be very rewarding.

I'd like to invite you on a journey of exploring what is going on inside your children's minds, bodies, and souls during the ten to twelve years that mark adolescence. Although I'm a trained psychologist and counselor, I think my best training has come at home—as I'll explain in just a moment!

The Family Counselor

I came home in a great mood but soon walked into a tornado. The group I had just spoken to was unusually responsive. They laughed in all the right places, whipped out the hankies just when I hoped they would, nodded their heads when I dropped in the insights—to be honest, it couldn't have gone better. I had an opportunity to talk with several couples afterward and really felt that I had made a difference in their lives. As a psychologist and speaker, I couldn't ask for more. That's why I came home feeling so great.

Now let me explain the tornado.

I live in Tucson, Arizona, the only place in the world where water costs more than gasoline. On my way back from the airport, I reached the outskirts of our development, where I was greeted by a little stream of water running down the street.

What idiot has this much money to burn? I thought to myself.

So imagine my, uh, pleasure when I followed that stream all the way to its source—the Leman outside faucet.

Obviously the kids had been playing with the hose. When they had finished, instead of turning off the faucet, they dropped the hose and thereby proceeded to water half the desert.

What sweet, sweet kids I have, and what tender, paternal thoughts I carried through the front door.

Actually my first words upon entering our hallway resembled a waterfall's roar: *"Who left the water running in front of the house?"*

There was a sudden dead silence, finally broken by my precious wife's voice: "Oh, he's home. The family counselor."

Man, was I slammed! And rightfully so. I put down my bags and did what I should have done in the first place: I went back outside, turned off the hose, came back inside, and hugged my family.

I share this story to illustrate that all families have their moments of tension, and anyone can have his times of imperfection and shortcoming, no matter how many letters appear after his name. I have learned as much from being wrong as I have learned from being right. I don't speak as a perfect authority but as one who has been on the journey of parenting adolescents for quite a while. I've learned I am just as capable as the next guy of saying exactly the wrong thing and hurting tender, budding teenage feelings by suggesting that a certain boy is special when my daughter would rather not talk about that just then.

Throughout this book, I want to be a kind friend who shares some of his stories about surviving the adolescence of his own children. Whatever you've lived through, I've probably experienced it myself. Because of my experience, however, I won't put you off with easy answers or a know-it-all attitude. One thing I *can* say, however, is that adolescence isn't terminal (it just feels like it). I've seen three kids come out on the other side, and if you go through this stage in the right way, believe me, there are tremendous rewards awaiting you as you relate to your adult children.

My goals are realistic. I jokingly told one group that the primary goal of getting our children through the teenage years is actually quite simple: to get them into their twenties without having them kill someone or being killed themselves! If they can avoid jail in the process, so much the better.

But seriously, the reason for this new book is simple: The kids we're raising now are from a different generation; old rules no longer apply. Let's look at "Planet Adolescence" in the new millennium.

Planet Adolescence 2001

When exactly do children enter that stage we call adolescence? I've got a good test for you. You know your sons or daughters are embarking on this period when you see them sink down into the car seat as you drive past some kids on the corner. As soon as you see this near universal moment, you know your children are entering that period in life when they desire to be free from parental restraint. It could begin when your children are as young as ten, and almost always strikes by the time they are twelve or thirteen. And when it happens, you know that for the next decade, you're going to be orbiting around Planet Adolescence.

While adolescence is something we've all experienced ourselves, we make a big mistake if we assume our children's experience will be just like our own. I'm probably not the only person who feels as if my kids turned thirteen on a planet different from the one I was born on.

During a four-year period, CBS conducted scientific polls of more than 2,300 students (from various high schools) scheduled to graduate in the year 2000; CBS also followed and interviewed 200 students more closely. The results were interesting–and sobering.

In 1997 a surprisingly large 43 percent knew of someone who had tried to commit suicide, a number that got even worse by graduation, with 70 percent of them knowing people who had tried to kill themselves.

As freshmen, less than 25 percent knew someone who was openly gay. As seniors, 66 percent did.

There were also some encouraging signs, including the fact that 46 percent of the students felt that their relationship with their parents had improved to excellent (up from 34 percent).[1] Unfortunately that still means more than half were not satisfied at home.

Another study found that illicit drug use doubles during the adolescent years. While 28.3 percent of surveyed teens admitted to using illegal drugs as eighth graders, over half– 54.7 percent–of the students in the twelfth grade made the same admission.[2] Yet another study found that 39 percent of students surveyed had used tobacco at least once by the end of seventh grade.[3]

In spite of these troubling statistics, today's teens are almost comically optimistic about their financial future. According to an Ernst and Young survey, 30 percent of college students polled expect to be millionaires in their forties. More than one in five expect to retire in their forties or earlier! More than 60 percent plan on retiring at a younger age than their parents did. If you can believe it, only 25 percent believe they will never be millionaires.[4]

Not only are today's kids a little more adventurous and a lot more optimistic than we were, but the things that would have made us blush as adolescents are second nature to them. While I served as assistant dean of students at the University of Arizona in the seventies, I saw my share of provocative girlie posters—but now women have posters of men striking roughly the same poses, something you never saw back then. I read with interest an Ann Landers column in which a mom complained that her fourteen-year-old son's girlfriend gave him a collage of pictures of naked women—including cutout photos of side, front, and rear views. Call me old, but fourteen-year-old girls didn't do that sort of thing when I was in junior high!

This can create almost humorous misunderstandings between the generations. I got a chuckle when professional tennis player Anna Kournikova—who at the time of this writing had yet to win a professional tournament but whose knockout looks have given her great fame—complained during a press conference organized to promote some undergarments that she endorses, "I'm not here to talk about my personal life. I'm here to talk about bras."

In the world many of us grew up in, husbands and wives couldn't be seen in the same bed on television, so producers created the marital double-bed set. Most of today's kids have already seen everything that goes on in bed—and the scenes on TV many times are not even between husbands and wives.

Planet Adolescence 2001 is in a different galaxy from the one we grew up in. Parenting rules that worked for your toddlers and preadolescents won't serve you well in this new age. For instance, when your kids were toddlers, you were able to control their environment so that many of the negative influences we just mentioned could be minimized. You could control what they watched on television and the friends with whom they played.

With adolescents, unfortunately, those days are gone. As we will see later, the days of controlling are over. You can still influence your children, but you can't control them.

You're also going to have to accept that your children may develop a different agenda for their lives than the one you've laid out for them. Adolescence is all about trying on independence—and that means your children will develop their own concerns.

Different Concerns

Along about age twelve—but perhaps as early as age ten—your children will start to grow away from you. They'll become more dependent on their peers, and in reaching toward adulthood, they may even act as if they regret ever having any association with such "uncool" parents.

This is a normal developmental stage that the wise parent will have fun with rather than resent. One time one of my daughters wanted to thank me for something, so she said, "I'll do anything you want!"

"Great!" I said. "Let's go walk around the mall together while I wear Bermuda shorts, black socks, and white tennis shoes!"

I soon found out that no teenage daughter's love extends *that* far! And to be honest, I didn't expect it to.

Also, about this age your teenagers' concerns will be different from your own. One recent study found that while parents and teens share the same top concern, other concerns diverge widely.[5] The following table illustrates the differing concerns. Each number represents how each group ranked their concerns. For example, both teens and parents ranked HIV and STDs as their number one concern. Teens then ranked drinking and driving as their number two concern, but parents listed it as their number nine concern, with car accidents as their number two concern.

Top Concerns	Teens	Parents
HIV and STDs (sexually transmitted diseases)	1	1
Drinking and driving	2	9
Pregnancy	3	4
Guns, knives, and other weapons	4	3
Suicide	5	17
Car accidents	7	2
Casual sex	12	5

Two things strike me about this poll. First, most parents are unaware of how much a topic suicide is among today's teens. That's a dangerous omission, which we'll thoroughly deal with later in this book. Second, notice that casual sex isn't even among the top ten concerns of today's youth. They don't see it as a problem—they view it as an opportunity! Once again, we're going to have to do some work here to help parents and teens come together.

The Girls Scouts of America commissioned a poll of girls ages eight to twelve—preadolescents—to determine their top concerns. Unfortunately the study revealed that most young girls today are preoccupied with body image and relationships. One respondent, a fifth grader, told researchers, "I've been counting calories. I'm doing 1,000 to 2,000 calories a day."

Just as sobering, the study found that while preteens want to talk to their parents about these issues, they often refrain from doing so because they believe "our parents do not want to hear about these issues." One fifth grader said, "All [my parents] say is I'm too young and I shouldn't even think about stuff like that until I am sixteen."[6]

This is what I'm talking about when I say you'll make a terrible mistake if you assume that the concerns you had as an adolescent will mirror the concerns weighing on your children's minds today. We're living in a different age and a different world. If you already have a great relationship with your preadolescent—fantastic! But you still will want to pay close attention to the advice in this book. I've seen so many relationships go sour within twelve months or less of a child's hitting puberty.

If your relationship has already been rocky, take heart! As a father I've steered several children through this tumultuous stage, and as a counselor I've worked with hundreds, perhaps thousands, of adolescent children. While I can't guarantee you smooth sailing, I can guarantee that adolescence isn't terminal—eventually those self-centered, insecure, independent-minded teens grow up into productive, caring, and balanced adults.

If in the midst of the struggle to raise your kid right, you wonder whether it's worth the effort, let me assure you that it is. Your son or daughter may grow up to affect millions of other lives—and the way you raise them could have a major impact on whether that influence is for good or for ill.

Let's look at the wildly divergent tales of two adults who have just recently passed through adolescence and are having an impact on their world.

A Tale of Two Teens

Marshall Mathers's father left home when Marshall was just six months old. Once Marshall became a teenager, he tried to contact his father, but his dad never replied. That left Marshall to make do with a mom who was filled with a lot of anger. A friend of Marshall's recalls how Marshall's mom came home from shopping one time, and after the boys helped unload the groceries, she told Marshall to get out, using plenty of expletives in the process.

According to the friend, "He'd get kicked out every week. There has not been a day in that house when there's not some kind of chaos."

You wouldn't expect much out of Marshall, would you? One magazine described him as a "scrawny white mullet-head from a broken home in a dead-end suburb of Detroit." Unfortunately Marshall Mathers, a.k.a. "Eminem" (as in "M and M"—*Marshall Mathers*), has become one of the most influential and successful rap singers of our day, described by one reporter as "the foul-mouthed prince of hate and fury."[7]

Eminem boldly and proudly proclaims that God sent him to make people angry. His manager, Paul Rosenberg, says that the rap star is getting angrier by the day: "He never lets water run off his back."[8]

The rapper deals with his anger toward his father in a public fashion. One of his rhymes goes like this: "When you see my dad, tell him I slit his throat in this dream I had."

I can't repeat the lyrics Marshall uses regarding his mom. They are too offensive even to report, some of the most vile things a son could say about his mother.

Marshall's wife, Kim, has had to endure this wealthy young star's anger as well. Eminem has a tattoo on his stomach with his wife's name, but it's hardly flattering: KIM: ROT IN PIECES. In several of his songs, Marshall talks about beating up and even killing his wife. After a performance in Detroit, in which Eminem was particularly vile, Kim left the hall, went home, and slit her wrists. Fortunately she was discovered and rescued by her mother and Marshall's half brother.[9]

Not surprisingly, Marshall's life is a mess. His mother has sued him, and at the time of this writing, Marshall and Kim are headed for a divorce.

Shockingly, Eminem is an award-winning performer who garnered three MTV awards in 2000. His *Marshall Mathers LP* is one of the best-selling hip-hop albums of all time, remaining on the *Billboard* Top Ten list for months. His hate-filled lyrics have found a raucous welcome from young adolescents all over this country. Eminem is leading our kids into a verbal filth unknown to previous generations.

What happened here? Without a dad and with a mom who

faced her own share of problems, Marshall grew up largely on his own, and the results speak for themselves. Adolescents don't "naturally" grow up into productive, law-abiding, respectful people.

Does that mean that every adolescent from a single-parent home is headed for trouble? By no means. Let's look at adolescent number two.

As a twentysomething superstar baseball player, shortstop Alex Rodriguez has a lot of things going for him—more money than he can spend, plenty of fame, people clamoring after his autograph, crowds yelling out his name, and little boys putting his poster on their bedroom walls.

But the world's adulation can never completely fill a cup left empty by a parent. That's why I was caught short when I heard Alex talking about one of the most significant events in his life. You see, until recently Alex hadn't seen his dad since the fourth grade. Though Alex's career was going well (he was chosen as the all-star shortstop during the 2000 season), he still felt a sense of loss because he was alienated from his dad.

I'll let Alex explain it in his own words, which he posted on his Web site.

My father left our family when I was in the fourth grade. I always thought he would come back, but he never did. It broke my young heart. I spoke with him over the phone a handful of times until my teen years. Then I closed my heart to him.

My family has pleaded with me over the years to reconcile. I constantly refused. Dad had tried in his own way to reach out to me as an adult. He approached me before a winter game just after I turned pro. I shook hands with him but couldn't say anything. I made it clear I didn't want to talk with him. It just hurt too much. The pain was too deep.

As I've grown as a professional baseball player, I've dealt

with the pressures of expectations, the pressures of performing in front of thousands, the pressures of a game on the
line. But when it came to my dad, I couldn't deal with the
pressure of seeing him face-to-face. . . .

Just before the turn of the millennium, a friend suggested
I seek out my father to start the new century with an open
heart. I brushed it off. Then the father of one of my former
coaches passed away. He had given me some words of
encouragement to reach out to my father. So when he
passed away, it hit home. Recently I've felt stronger. I've
made some strides personally. So I figured, what the heck,
I'll go for it.

So, I called my dad and invited him to our series in
Minnesota. He showed up! And we spent a few days
together. It was the first time he'd seen me play in the
Major Leagues in person. It was great. . . . Father's Day
was perfect. My on-field gift to him was going four-for-five
with a home run.

We met for the first time in a very private fashion. I
was nervous. And I could tell he was nervous. We shook
hands and then hugged. And then we talked about a lot
of things.[10]

As a wealthy, successful baseball player, Alex has the world at
his feet. He is adored, cheered, and catered to, but none of that
could completely still the sense of loss represented by an absent
father. Many boys dream about making it to the big leagues, but
"Arod" is one big leaguer who spent his time dreaming about
making it back to being with his dad.

Here's my point: During adolescence your children may act as
if you are the least significant person on the face of the planet.
They may treat you as if you are nothing more than a nuisance, a
bother, and a big pain—but in their hearts, they are crying out for
your attention, your love, your concern, and even your guidance.

The trick is learning to provide that attention, love, concern, and guidance in a way that your kids can receive them.

Marshall Mathers and Alex Rodriguez are good reminders that today's kids become tomorrow's headlines. Some will work for good causes, raise families of their own, and be productive members of our society. Others will attack, assault, and create havoc wherever they go.

A number of self-help books have stressed how important it is, in the words of Steven Covey, to "begin with the end in mind." That is, we should start a project with a view toward the intended outcome. I think that's pretty good advice for raising kids. What kind of kids do you want to have? Do you want to raise selfish kids who whine and moan and get by in life doing as little as they can? Or do you want to raise kids who contribute to society, live out their faith, and leave behind a proud legacy?

If you think ahead of time about who you want your kids to be when they reach adulthood, you stand a much better chance of making it through the murky atmosphere of Planet Adolescence.

Our Road Map

Here's where we're headed on this journey through today's adolescence. We'll begin our exploration running. I know that some of you are desperate, so I'm putting the most basic and concise information right up front. Chapter 2 gives you twenty rules for surviving your children's adolescence.

In chapters 3 and 4 we'll explore the power of peer pressure, talking first about how peer pressure percolates (hint: the process starts when your children are still babies!) and then about how to steer your adolescent through it. In chapter 5 I challenge you to provide the most stable home life possible, giving your children what some now refer to as "the fairy-tale lifestyle." Chapter 6 looks at how to pass on the values we believe in, and chapter 7 will help you navigate those everyday hassles of living with adolescents.

In chapter 8 I'll talk about how raising adolescents is a risky business. This chapter might make some of you a little anxious—but you need to hear what I have to say. In chapter 9 I take on the topic of toxic parents, exploring parenting styles that are guaranteed to blow up in your face once your children reach their teens. After reading this chapter, you'll be aptly warned.

From there chapter 10 provides some of my most unorthodox advice, followed by chapter 11, which deals with love and dating. Since many parents tell me they need help dealing with their adolescents' sexual issues, I have included two chapters about sex and the adolescent. Chapter 12 helps you talk to your teens about sex, especially about sexual abstinence, and chapter 13 discusses some of the more delicate aspects of teen sexual expression. The final chapter looks at the troublesome issues that all parents want their teens to avoid: suicide, substance abuse, eating disorders, hate groups, and the like.

We've got a lot of ground to cover, so let's get started.

Remember:

- Adolescence is a much different experience for our kids from what it was for us.
- "Good" kids and "bad" kids both share the same deep desire: They want a real, deep, and meaningful relationship with their parents.
- The best way to steer our kids through the stage of adolescence is to know ahead of time what type of children we want to raise.

2

Twenty Rules for Surviving Your Kids' Adolescence

ADOLESCENTS ARE FAMOUS FOR wanting the best of both worlds. On Friday night they say, "Get out of my life, leave me alone, give me space!" On Saturday morning they say, "Hey, Mom and Dad, take care of me. Every time I get in a hassle or need a few extra bucks, I want you to bail me out."

What's going on?

In a word: *hormones*. Adolescents live on emotions. One day they're sky high, skiing down the slopes of Mount Everest. The next day they've plunged into Death Valley. This topsy-turvy existence comes with a huge price tag: adolescents are notorious for hurting those who are closest to them.

Flip on a television station at midday, and you're likely to hear some psychologist tell a clapping audience, "If we just love our kids enough, everything will work out okay." I wish it were that simple. Unfortunately it's not. Love is not complete without discipline. While our kids need lots of encouragement and positive reinforcement, they also need structure and guidelines.

We must be careful not to equate discipline with punishment.

Discipline means to teach, to disciple, to show the way. Parents need to give guidelines, set limits, establish rules, and enforce them. Sometimes that may involve punishment.

When I recently appeared on *The View*, I mentioned the importance of letting kids suffer the consequences of their actions, even if that means not covering for them at school.

"You mean you'd rat on your own kid?" one of the hosts asked, incredulous.

"Yes, I would," I said.

"Boooo!" she hissed.

I think this host suffers from "good parent complex," something I see so often in my counseling practice. These parents have a difficult time enforcing rules and regulations for fear their children might reject them. In fact, it sends the opposite signal. Guidelines are important because they communicate to our children that we care what happens to them. The kids may not always agree with our guidelines, but that's all right. They also need something to bounce off of, to resist, if you will, because resistance is what builds strength. Regulations that teenagers resist will help keep them on a course that is instructive, not destructive, and will help them build the muscle they will need when they are on their own, making their own decisions. For their own sake, children must be taught to respect and obey parental authority.

Healthy children exist on three pillars of understanding:

1. They have to respect and obey their parents.
2. They need to gain ownership of the belief that they are special people.
3. They should expect the best life has to offer them.

"That's all fine, Dr. Leman," some of you might be saying, "but how do I get these truths across?"

Fair enough. I'm going to give you twenty tried-and-true steps that will help you keep open the lines of communication with your children. These twenty steps represent the summation of what I believe will create the healthiest home for today's teens.

1. Follow Through

"Now listen, Gabe," Monica told her son, "if you don't have the garage cleaned out by Saturday, you're not going on that hike you and your buddies have planned."

"Okay, Mom," Gabe said.

Saturday morning rolls around, and Gabe has his backpack by the door. Monica takes a peek inside the garage and sees that her son hasn't even touched it. The recycling bins are turned over, grass clippings trail behind the lawn mower, and assorted sports equipment covers the floor.

"What happened to cleaning the garage?" Monica asked.

"Oh, sorry. I guess I forgot. I'll do it when I get back though, I promise."

"Oh, all right," Monica answers. "Just this one time, I'll let you off the hook. Have a good time."

Monica committed a cardinal error. If you say something is going to happen by way of discipline, be sure it happens. Don't say anything unless you intend to follow through. There are few worse mistakes parents can make than announcing consequences of a bad decision and then not following through on those consequences.

What you are doing when you don't follow through is teaching your children that your word doesn't really mean a thing. You're also telling them that they could carve a spine out of a banana and that spine would be firmer than the one inside your skin. When they find that out, they'll never stop taking advantage of you, obeying your word only when it's convenient. And now that your kids are adolescents, they have much more power and many more opportunities to exploit your weakness.

For your children's sake, think before you threaten. If major decisions need to be made, sleep on them a night or two and talk about them with your spouse before you settle on consequences. Don't let yourself be rushed into making a decision or giving your permission. Once you do agree on an appropriate set of consequences, hold to them.

2. Watch Your Expectations

"All Susan brings home are Bs and an occasional C. I just know she can do better that that," said a mother in my counseling office.

"Does she do her homework?" I asked.

"Yes, she's very responsible that way. But the grades just aren't there, and if she doesn't bring them up, she'll have to settle for community college instead of university."

"Does her teacher think she's slacking off?"

"No. Actually her teacher says she's performing about where she should, given her IQ, but Bob and I just can't accept that. Both of us were straight-A students."

Sharp adults can sometimes make overly demanding parents. Listen: It's a physiological fact that intelligence always runs to average. Even two very smart parents are likely to have a child with just average intelligence. One child might exceed the rest, but pedigree is not a guarantee that high IQ will be passed on.

Many times parents unknowingly place unrealistic expectations on their children. Your standards need to be realistic. You can't impose super-high expectations for your children and maintain an encouraging home life.

Unfortunately we live in a perfectionistic world. We are great at picking out the flaws in our children at the same time we take their strengths for granted. If we're not careful, our children will begin feeling like pets or showpieces rather than sons or daughters.

3. Accept Them Where They Are

It's tough to accept your children where they are. We don't have problems accepting other people's children where they are, but we know how we want our children to be, how we want them to think and act, and what we want them to achieve. When they fail to live up to our expectations, we become disappointed or take it personally.

Your goal as a parent is to help your children become all that they can be. It is not to make them feel guilty for not becoming what they aren't capable of becoming. If your children love to play baseball but aren't driven to practice, perfectly content with a .200 batting average, accept the fact that it's okay to play baseball for the fun of it without having to make the all-star team.

Also, be sensitive to your adolescents' stage of development. Although they may have the voice of an adult and the stature of an adult, your seventeen-year-old son is still in many respects a boy. Although your daughter fills out her blouse and could stop traffic on a sidewalk, she is still, in many ways, a little girl. Expect a certain amount of immaturity. Hyperbole, for example, is a way of life for teenagers: "I'll never fall in love again!" "You hate me, don't you?" "You just want to ruin my life!" These phrases have, at one time or another, passed the lips of most adolescents.

> Your goal as a parent is to help your children become all that they can be.

Try to recognize that your children have a right to their feelings. Hear them out, accept them as they are, and go on from there. If they are immature in the way they think, the best thing you can do is work hard to understand where they are coming from and accept them anyway. This will help them sort out their feelings, even if they never totally agree with you.

4. Take Time to Listen

You've got two ears and one mouth. Good parents take the hint in God's design and listen twice as much as they talk. If you want a relationship with your children, if you want to still be friends with your children when they become adults, take time to listen. Listening means that all your energy is geared toward just trying to hear and feel what your children are telling you. Don't be judgmental, and don't spend your listening time preparing what you're going to say when your adolescents are finished. *Really* listen. Force yourself to slow down.

Listening includes fitting yourself into your children's schedule. On many mornings our oldest daughter, Holly, and I read the newspaper together, about midmorning. Holly likes to sleep in, so if I am puttering around, we spend a good number of midmornings together. We chat about national and international news and get to know each other pretty well. Since Holly is a night owl, however, we have our best talks late at night. She can sleep through lunch and not think anything about it. Bedtime is the best time to talk to Holly.

Little Lauren, on the other hand, is usually the first one awake, and she treasures early morning cuddle time with her father. I get up, make a pot of coffee, watch the pre-*Today* show, and Lauren will find me, snuggle into my lap, and then say, "Daddy, can we change the channel?" Most of the time I'll say, "Sure." After watching a Disney show for a while and scratching Lauren's back, I'll cook her some eggs, then drop her off at school. Some of our best conversations happen in the car on the way to school.

So you see, listening involves not just sitting in front of your children but also finding out what time of the day they are most likely to open up and then being there during that time. Each child is different. Good managers adjust themselves to each of their employees; the same thing is true with good parents. Trying to have an intense breakfast discussion with a night owl will create only frustration and anger, not goodwill.

5. Respect Their Choices

This is a tough one, isn't it? After all, we know what clothes look best on our children; we know what friends they should be hanging around with; we know what activities they should engage in. We know everything our children should do, say, and be. Why can't they just submit and let us live their lives?

One night our son, Kevin, then fifteen years old, announced at the dinner table that he was going to get an earring. I looked at Sande, she looked at me, and we nonverbally agreed to let the comment pass. But of course it was too rich for me to ignore altogether, so the next time our family sat down for dinner, guess who was wearing one of his wife's earrings?

> It helps immensely if you can use humor and be playful about some of these issues.

You got it.

At first Kevin didn't notice my accessory at all as he focused on wolfing down his dinner. All of a sudden his eyes narrowed, he stared at my head, and then said, "You look absolutely ridiculous."

I made a hand motion, as if I were pumping up my hair, and said, "Really? Well, your mother likes it."

That ended any desire on Kevin's part to put another hole in his head!

In all honesty, however, neither Sande nor I would have forbidden Kevin from getting an earring. They're his ears, after all. If he wants to put a tin can on one of them, he's welcome to. I'm not going to major in the minors.

Depending on your personality as a parent, it helps immensely if you can use humor and be playful about some of these issues. Lots of times they work themselves out, and they don't need to become major or even minor hassles.

One of the toughest assignments for us parents is to respect our children and their choices. We sometimes assume they'll always make the wrong choices—and for a time, they might. But if we raise them right, they'll come back to wisdom in the long run. There were some interesting studies done of elementary-age children who were allowed to eat anything they wanted in a school cafeteria during a month of testing. Of course, at the beginning of the month-long experiment the children pigged out on the desserts, sweets, and all the goodies. But as the days marched by, they began to swing back to a very traditional and well-balanced diet.

Adolescents in particular love to test us. They are going to purposefully try things that they know we don't like just to see if we will love them even when we disagree with them. A Republican committeeman shouldn't be surprised when his high school son comes home sporting a button for a Democratic candidate. Kids want us to respect their choices and listen to their opinions. In fact, it's this desire for respect that is behind much of the rebellion that occurs during the teen years. Right or wrong, kids want their opinions to be heard, taken seriously, and respected.

Trust me on this one: I've talked to numerous parents who took this advice to heart only to discover that when their kids were grown, they became more like their mother and father than the parents ever would have hoped for or thought. In fact, I know of one Republican senator—who shall remain nameless, thank you very much—whose once Democrat-leaning adolescent now (in his late twenties) routinely scolds his dad for being too *liberal*.

6. Ask for Forgiveness

"Love means never having to say you're sorry."

This nutty catchphrase from the seventies still crops up in my counseling room from time to time, and it's dead wrong. Too many parents feel they should never have to ask for forgiveness from their children because they believe that as parents they are somehow "superior." No way! We all fall short; we all occasionally blow it. And when we do, we should model the proper response, which means saying the words "I'm sorry. Will you forgive me?"

I've seen the most rebellious kids imaginable melt like butter when Dad or Mom finally says, "I've been way too harsh with you. Please forgive me." While we may think that our children will not respect us if we admit that we were insensitive, cruel, mean, or forgetful, we need to see that our confession really makes us stand tall in our teenagers' eyes. Asking for forgiveness opens up any number of avenues for our children to share with us.

7. Respect Their Privacy

Emotions are gushing with the force of Niagara Falls through your adolescents' bodies. Sexual feelings are running rampant. Your teenagers are trying to get a feel for who they are. Because of this, your kids need you to step back and let them have their privacy. It's hard to handle the fact that your little boy or little girl doesn't want to crawl into your lap anymore or go for a ride in the family car or do much of anything with the family. You may even get the feeling that your teenagers are interested only in having a bunk at the house and some food on the table to keep them going so they can continue their busy social life, talk on the phone constantly, and attend to their duties at school. But in the midst of this, they're building their independence while still under the shelter of your love and concern. Help them by respecting their privacy.

8. Communicate Clearly

Because adolescents and adults grow up in different generations, the potential for misunderstanding and miscommunication is high. Small disagreements or even simple misunderstandings can quickly escalate into vicious battles. Don't let that happen. Learn how to communicate and listen so that you don't face what happened to a church I know.

A small country church struggled for over a year to buy a new chandelier for the sanctuary. They had a promotional campaign and already had the approval of the committee in charge of church expenditures. But according to the church bylaws, an expenditure of this magnitude had to be approved by 100 percent of the church congregation.

The committee chairman stood up and asked for the final vote. Everybody except one old farmer voted to buy the chandelier. The chairman went over how much a new chandelier was needed, and then called for another vote. Once again the farmer was the only one withholding his approval.

Frustrated to no end, the chairman finally asked the farmer why he was the only one who didn't want to buy the chandelier.

The old fellow replied, "There's too many other things this church needs, like a light in the sanctuary."

There was a gasp, a few snickers, and then the chairman carefully defined what a chandelier is. The next vote, of course, passed unanimously.

Speak clearly to your kids. Be honest. Make sure you understand each other.

9. Do the Unexpected

It's been a long day for both of you. Everybody has wanted something from you at work. You come home exhausted and hungry. There wasn't any time for lunch, so you can't wait to get some food into your stomach. You remember that on Wednesdays it's your children's job to have dinner ready. You can taste the taco salad that they had planned to prepare.

Walking through the door, you don't smell dinner cooking or hear any dishes rattling, but you do hear the sound of Oprah Winfrey on television. You walk into the kitchen and find that not only is dinner not prepared but the breakfast dishes haven't even been done!

In most homes across America, the next scene would be this: Mom and Dad would rant and rave, and the kids would reluctantly get up off the couch. Then Mom and Dad would follow them, roll up their sleeves, and help them prepare dinner. If you do this, you better be prepared to make it a weekly ritual because your children will never change if you let them off the hook.

I've got a much better solution. As soon as you survey the sad shape of the kitchen, grab your car keys, meet your spouse outside, and go out to dinner, just the two of you, letting your kids fend for themselves. I would repeat this procedure until the children finally do as they were told to do.

"But, Dr. Leman, wouldn't that get a little expensive?"

Ah, here's the fun part. When you come home, you post the restaurant bill on the refrigerator. When the kids ask you what the bill is doing there, you say, "Well, you guys didn't have dinner ready for us, so we went out to dinner. But there's no reason we should have to pay for what you failed to do, so this amount, plus the tip, will be taken out of your next allowance."

> We need to hold children responsible for what we expect of them.

"But that's more than three weeks' allowance!"

"It sure is. You didn't think we were going to go out to a fast-food restaurant after a long day at work, did you? By the way, we've got our eyes on this great Italian restaurant that's just opening up downtown. We can't wait until you guys spend all afternoon watching television again so that we can get another free dinner!"

I can practically guarantee that you'll have this conversation only once! It'll be a lesson that your kids will never forget. Never again will you have to worry about whether they are responsible about getting dinner ready. The weekly fights will be over.

The point is, we need to hold children responsible for what

we expect of them. That's our responsibility as parents. We can't beat them over the heads and make them do things, but we also can't play into their hands. Doing the "unexpected" creates a long-lasting shock value.

10. Talk about Potential Problems

Dad finds out that sixteen-year-old Jennifer is about to go out on her first one-on-one date. In a panic he steps inside her bedroom as she works on her hair.

"Big date, huh?" he asks.

Jennifer blushes.

Now Dad is *really* nervous. "Well, you know, Jennifer, boys can be, uh, well, they can, sometimes, you know . . ."

Jennifer looks at him as if he's lost his mind—an understandable reaction, since Dad sounds as if he did!

"Well, Jennifer, you see, guys are different from girls, so, well, you just need to be careful."

"Okay, Dad."

"I'm glad we had this talk, Jennifer."

What was accomplished in that conversation? Absolutely nothing. Dad is about five years too late. It is really important to talk to your children about some of the pitfalls and challenges that lie before them well before they get there. Talking to thirteen- or fourteen-year-olds about when they begin dating at sixteen is, in my opinion, a good thing to do. A thirteen-year-old—I would hope—isn't feeling quite as much pressure to date as a sixteen-year-old is, so your communication can go much deeper. Your teenagers won't be so emotional about the situation and thus will be more likely to carefully consider what you have to say.

Talking to your kids ahead of time will also give them plenty of time to think at leisure about the decisions that are ahead of them, allowing them to make rational decisions about whether or not they'll go parking—before they're looking at gorgeous Julie or Mark with those piercing blue eyes. It will fortify them against the intense pressure that arises when children are presented with their first joint of marijuana or fifth of whiskey in the backseat of a friend's car.

The day before—or the day of—the first date is much too late. Chapters 11 and 12 will help you think through the dating issue and talk to your teens about things they should know.

11. Don't Act like a Teenager

It's a temptation for many of us to feel that by not acting our age, we identify with our children and make them feel comfortable with us. Actually the reverse is true. Kids who have parents who try to act, look, and talk like teenagers tell me that they feel very self-conscious and embarrassed when their moms or dads attempt to be teenagers. Most adolescents want us to act, look, and talk like parents. That's our role. They have plenty of buddies; they need parents. There is a difference.

12. Give Them Choices

Life as an adult is full of choices. Whenever my car gets dirty, I have to ask myself, *Should I spend an hour on Saturday washing and waxing my car, or should I pay nine dollars at the car wash?* There's no right answer to that question; it's a matter of preference and life-style.

If your teenagers are complaining about having to mow the lawn instead of going skateboarding, give them the choice: "Hey, it's up to you. You can pay little Jimmy down the street eight bucks to mow the lawn, or you can do it yourself. It doesn't matter to me, as long as it gets done. Just remember, if *I* have to do it, I charge a lawyer's rate."

"What's that?"

"Two hundred and fifty dollars an hour."

This method gets our teenagers a little closer to life's realities. There are real responsibilities in the world, yet different ways to handle each one of them. Home is the safest place for our adolescents to learn how to make these decisions.

13. Don't Snowplow Their School Road

When you get involved in kids' schoolwork and activities, 90 percent of the time that involvement is negative involvement.

You read that right. It's important that teenagers learn early in their childhood that their education is their own responsibility and no one else's.

Actually even kindergartners don't want their parents to be too obvious around their school. One mother I know was going on a field trip with her son's kindergarten class. The little boy said, "Please don't sit near me." Children want their school life separate from their home life.

This is not to say that parents should not give children encouragement in their homework or that they shouldn't see that their teenagers set aside time to do their homework; but parents should resist the temptation to help them with it or do it for them or try in any way to make it easier for them.

I realize that this is a very politically incorrect position to take; in fact, even your schools may not agree with me! I once worked with a father who literally had to beat on the high school principal's desk to get him to flunk his freshman son. All of the boy's grades for the entire year were Ds and Fs. It was clear he hadn't learned anything, yet the school authorities had the audacity to say they were going to promote him to the next grade because they thought it would be bad for him to stay back with younger children.

How are we ever going to teach accountability and responsibility to children when our system tells them that no matter what they do or how badly they fail, they'll pass anyway?

14. Don't Show Them Off or Embarrass Them

Every family has at least one kid who's talented, clever, cute, or outstanding in some way. Some people have a whole houseful of kids like that. But please, spare the kids and your friends—don't embarrass the kids by making them show off.

The kids aren't fooled. They know you're taking credit, and they don't like being treated like "monkeys" who perform when given a few peanuts just so you can have everyone pat you on the back and tell you what a nice job of parenting you've done.

It's understandable and natural to be proud of your children's accomplishments, and there are appropriate ways to express that. Whatever you do, don't put your violin-playing or gymnastic-tumbling children on the spot by asking them to perform for others without preparing them. You wouldn't like someone to do that to you. Why would you do that to your teenagers?

The other side of this is, don't embarrass them. When your teenagers goof up or disappoint you, it's very tempting to brow-beat them in front of their peers. How would you feel if someone did that to you? You wouldn't want to be ridiculed or laughed at before your peers by someone you love, so have the courtesy to wait until you're alone with your teenagers. Then if they need chewing out, fine! A good chewing out never hurts—just make sure it's done in the appropriate time and place.

15. Don't Pick at Flaws

The teens I talk to in my counseling room are painfully aware of their shortcomings. They think they're too fat, too dumb, too ugly, too stupid, and too clumsy to ever amount to anything. I'm not just talking about the "losers." I'm also talking about relatively popular kids who still seem almost consumed by their inadequacies. They make ridiculous comparisons: the thin girl wonders why she doesn't wear a D-cup bra, while the girl who wears the D cup envies the thin girl's thighs. The wide receiver wishes he could play golf; the golfer wishes he were big enough to be a football player.

Trust me on this one: Teens see enough flaws in themselves and even magnify ones that barely exist. They don't need parents pouncing on every little thing they do. Self-esteem is usually at an all-time low during adolescence, and the unknowing parent can whittle away at what little positive self-image the adolescent has. Adolescents need to be reminded and encouraged to do what they should, but they don't need someone to constantly point out their weaknesses, failures, and flaws.

16. Don't Spit in Their Soup

"Mom, can I go to the game tonight?"

"I guess so, honey, but you know how much I worry when you're out past dark."

"Dad, can I go to the movies with Jim?"

"Sure, Son. At least one of us can have fun tonight. I'll stay home and weed the flower beds by myself."

"Spitting in your adolescent's soup" is when you add a little tagalong that has no other purpose than to make your teen feel guilty. If a dad wants his son to help him weed the flower beds, he should say so up front, rather than indirectly play the role of the martyr. If a mom doesn't want her daughter to be out past dark, but the daughter is old enough to do it, the mom should learn to keep her fears to herself instead of ruining her daughter's fun. Spitting in the soup is a sure way to create "the guilties" in your children and create a divisive relationship between you and your son or daughter.

A Bible verse is relevant here to parents of all faiths: Let your yes be yes and your no be no (see Matthew 5:37). If you don't want your children to go somewhere, don't let them. If you do decide to let them go, let them go—without making them feel guilty. One or the other; it's that simple!

17. Don't Talk in Volumes

In the late 1930s a young golf instructor had the formidable task of trying to teach the game to the renowned physicist Albert Einstein. The instructor had all the eagerness of youth without the wisdom of age, so it must have been a sight seeing this young man trying to help Einstein develop a swing.

Unfortunately what Einstein had in mental ability he seemed to lack in physical dexterity. His hand-eye coordination wasn't the best, and Einstein kept missing many of his shots. After each miss, the golf pro dutifully pointed out what Einstein had done wrong.

"Take the club back more slowly."

"Choke up on the club."

"Keep your head down."

"Don't open up the club face."

"You're jerking the club when you transition into the down-swing."

Finally an obviously frustrated Einstein asked the young golf pro to hand him a few balls, which the pro did. Then, throwing four balls back to the pro at once, Einstein yelled, "Catch!"

The pro dodged and weaved but failed to catch a single ball.

Einstein raised his finger and offered, "Young man, if I throw you just one ball, you can catch it. If I throw four at once, you can't catch even one. So when you teach, make only one point at a time!"

Einstein's admonition—make only one point at a time!—is good advice for parents of adolescents.

Well-meaning parents can be the worst at this, frankly. Many of us just wait for an opening as innocent as "What time is it?" to bring down volumes of advice and instructions. Listen, your kids are already in school five days a week; they can take in only so much. Let them enjoy shopping for a new pair of skis without your needing to explain the laws of aerodynamics.

I don't want to make every instance in life a "teachable" moment with my kids. For instance, if Hannah forgets her lunch and if I'm already going in the general direction of her school, I'll drop it off—without giving her a lecture. Everybody forgets things sometimes, and people who love each other help each other out. Now, if Hannah were forgetting her lunch four times a week, that would be a different story. For merely occasional lapses, however, I want to give my children the same courtesy I'd give anyone else—a helping hand without a boring lecture.

Instead of speaking in volumes, provide simple examples. For instance, I like to treat my kids by occasionally stopping at a Burger King and bringing a hot lunch to their school. One time Hannah specifically asked me to do this, and I agreed.

"What time do you guys break for lunch?" I asked.

"Eleven-thirty," Hannah said.

I stopped at a Burger King and bought two cheeseburgers, with an extra large order of fries, and arrived at Hannah's school precisely at 11:30.

Much to my surprise, the kids were still seated. Now, I've had enough fast food to know that it has a shelf life of about fifteen minutes. It tastes great when it's hot; it's okay when it's warm; but cold, mushy fries aren't on the top of anybody's list. So I started pacing outside of Hannah's room like a caged animal, waiting for her to get out.

Finally at 11:39, kids started streaming out of the classroom, making their way toward the cafeteria.

I'm standing outside, holding the Burger King bag, when a spunky girl sees me, stops short, turns to her friend, and announces, "Boy, I wish *my* dad delivered."

What do you say to *that?*

Hannah finally came out. I greeted her and said, "Hi, Hannah, how you doing, sweetie? By the way, I thought your lunch was at eleven thirty."

"Oh, sorry, it's *around* eleven thirty."

"Well, sorry, but your cheeseburgers are probably getting cold."

Hannah gratefully took the bag, then asked, "Why'd you get me two? You know I only eat one."

"Don't you think it'd be a good idea to let somebody else be a little extra happy today?"

"Gotcha. Thanks, Dad."

Hannah gave me a hug and a kiss and went on her way. Without delivering a sermon, I told Hannah how important it is to be aware of her friends and learn how to be thoughtful.

18. Don't Smother Them with Praise

I realize that most of us grew up feeling that praise was important. In fact, I've seen bumper stickers that say "Look for the good, and praise it." It sounds great, but I've found that praise can be a very defeating thing for adolescents. Let me try to explain.

I see a distinction between praise and encouragement. I know that sounds like a subtle distinction to you, but it's important. Both are verbal, but *praise* inflates and attaches worth to people *because* of what they do, while *encouragement* expresses genuine appreciation for who people are.

Here's a good example of a typical case of praise. Carol comes home from a long day of shopping and is pleasantly surprised to find that her thirteen-year-old daughter cleaned up the kitchen. Shocked and in disbelief, Carol exclaims, "Shelly, come here! What a sweetheart you are! I love you so much for doing this! You are an incredible daughter!"

What is this mother communicating? She is implying that she loves her daughter because of something she did and that her worth is tied to her performance.

Let's look at what encouragement would look like in this same situation. Carol walks into the clean, sparkling kitchen and says, "Shelly, did you clean the kitchen? It's a joy to come home and see it so neat and sparkling. I just want you to know how much I appreciate your thoughtfulness. Thank you." She then gives Shelly a hug.

What does this encouragement communicate? It communicates to Shelly that her mom noticed what she did and that she appreciates her thoughtfulness. But notice that the emphasis is on her thoughtfulness (who she is) and not on the job (what she did).

The danger of praising adolescents is that they might view

themselves as being loved or prized or appreciated because they do the dishes or get good grades or excel in sports, and that isn't true. We love our adolescents regardless of whether or not they do extra work or get all A's or win a championship.

Let's see how praise and encouragement look in another scenario. Jeff has a solid night on the basketball court, and by the end of the game he has racked up twenty-eight points. His dad is in the stands, hollering and cheering him on. After the game Jeff's dad approaches him, slaps him on the back, and says loudly enough for Jeff's teammates to hear, "Man, Jeff, you were awesome. You are on the way to getting that scholarship for sure. I am one happy father. Did you see that scout in the stands? You are NBA material, Son. No doubt about it."

Now some of you might say, "What's wrong with that? The dad is proud of his son. He's a little enthusiastic, and maybe he gets carried away a bit. But is that bad?"

I think it is. Jeff's dad seems to be measuring his son's worth by his performance. He inflates his son's expectations by announcing that Jeff must be on his way to the NBA. That's a lot of pressure. What happens when Jeff scores only eight points the next game? Will his dad still rave? Will his dad be disappointed? Will he be one unhappy father?

What would encouragement look like in this same situation? "Jeff, you had a great night out there, Son. That must have felt good. You really helped out your team tonight. I'm glad I was here to share your excitement." He puts his arm around Jeff and gives his shoulder a squeeze.

Jeff is encouraged to know his dad was there to share his team's win and that his dad understands what it feels like to have a good night. But I don't think Jeff feels that if he doesn't do this well at the next game, his dad will be disappointed. Jeff doesn't feel that pressure. He knows that his dad loves him because he is his son, whether he scores twenty-eight points or eight points.

As I said before, this is a hard difference to see at first, but I encourage you to listen to yourself when you are giving your adolescents verbal feedback. Are you praising (inflating, measuring worth by performance) or encouraging (expressing genuine appreciation for who your kids are)?

I don't want my kids to become dependent on verbal carrots, always needing people to give them "strokes." What will happen when there aren't others around to praise them constantly? What happens when your adolescents become adults and can't find substitute mothers or dads to give them strokes? If they're dependent on these verbal carrots, they'll fall apart. They won't be able to handle things well when they're not praised. I want kids who will be self-motivated and who will take responsibility for their own lives, even if it is difficult.

> I want kids who will be self-motivated and who will take responsibility for their own lives, even if it is difficult.

Michael J. Fox, the well-known young actor who shocked the nation when he announced that he has Parkinson's disease, said something very profound in an interview he gave to *George* magazine: "When you have a long-term illness, you . . . see things differently. People grieve so much about being misunderstood. 'Nobody understands me.' Well, you know what? They're not going to. The person who loves you more than anyone in the world thinks about you, purely, ten seconds if you're lucky. I'm not being derogatory. It's simply that you are responsible for your own experience."[1]

I'm not used to hearing such insight from the mouth of a Hollywood movie star! In the real world our kids won't always be noticed. No one will see them do the small, responsible things like pay their bills on time, quietly support their family, or mow their own lawn. They need to become self-motivating, and overuse of praise works against that.

19. Don't Make Icebergs out of Icicles

Do you ever make a mistake? Have you ever had a season at work where you aced three projects and did mediocre work on the fourth? Have you ever done your best to cook the perfect dinner, only to make a mess of it? I bet you have, so let me ask you a question: Will you extend to your children the same grace that you extend to yourself?

Here's what I'm talking about. What do you say when your son hands you his report card and he has three A's and one C? Do you get red in the face, grab your throat, and scream, "Oh no, a C! What's with this C?" A far better approach would be to say, "Three A's and a C! I'm really glad to see you enjoy learning. I'll bet you're proud of your effort."

I work hard at everything I do, but I have off days just as my kids do. Sometimes when I'm doing a radio show, I'll feel as if I'm in a "zone." Appropriate analogies come to mind right away; humor slips out of me unbidden; no questions leave me stumped. Other days, I stumble over words, try a joke that fails, and get a little windy with my answers.

With this in mind, I regard three A's and a C to be an excellent report card. Very few of us bat a thousand, even though many parents feel compelled to focus on the C and ignore the A.

Give your children grace. A spilled glass of Coke isn't rebellion; it's clumsiness. Instead of giving them a lecture, hand them a dishcloth and let them clean up the spill. Leaving the milk out too long is certainly annoying, but it's not a federal offense.

It's your choice. Are you going to make your home a place of acceptance, encouragement, and support, or turn it into a house filled with pressure, expectations, and perfectionism?

20. Handle Hassles Healthily

I can give you just one absolutely foolproof, money-back guarantee about living with an adolescent: you will have conflicts. When (not if) a hassle develops and you're feeling that uneasiness between you and your adolescent, approach the situation with a positive attitude. Pick an appropriate time and place (i.e., not in front of their friends or when they're too emotional to discuss anything objectively) where both of you are comfortable and can discuss the conflict maturely.

First, give your teenagers the opportunity to explain their side of things. For example, if your daughter has thrown flour all over her younger sister, begin by saying, "I'm very interested in what you were thinking and feeling when you threw flour at your sister." After your daughter describes her feelings and explains her reactions, *take time out to reason, think, and pause* before you jump into an answer. Make sure you understand exactly what she is trying to say.

Next, ask her to listen to your point of view. Try to be as specific as you can about why you're bothered by the fact that your youngest daughter looks like an apple pie with arms. Don't be general. All that does is leave room for misinterpretation and inaccuracy. Get very specific: "I understand that you must have been very frustrated when Samantha added an extra cup of flour to your mix, but pouring it over her head isn't a proper response for a thirteen-year-old. What do you think would have been a better response?"

You handle hassles healthily when you work toward a mutual solution to the problem. There may need to be some compromise and negotiation, but that's true of everything in life—you're helping your adolescents to function as adults. If there is any doubt in your mind or in your adolescents' minds as to what is expected the next time little sis makes a nuisance of herself, take the time to write out the agreement and sign it. That way, if there's ever any need to go back and refer to it, everyone knows exactly what was expected.

There you have them. Twenty rules that will help you survive your years of parenting adolescents. If parents would simply practice these twenty rules, there would be far fewer families finding their way into my counseling room or others' offices. Big problems often arise when we ignore the little things.

But there is much more to raising adolescents than merely following a few nuggets of homespun wisdom. Adolescence forces us to tackle pressing issues, including one that concerns virtually every parent: peer pressure. Let's turn our attention to this topic in the next chapter.

Remember:

- Follow through.
- Watch your expectations.
- Accept them where they are.
- Take time to listen.
- Respect their choices.
- Ask for forgiveness.
- Respect their privacy.
- Communicate clearly.
- Do the unexpected.
- Talk about potential problems.
- Don't act like a teenager.
- Give them choices.
- Don't snowplow their school road.
- Don't show them off or embarrass them.
- Don't pick at flaws.
- Don't spit in their soup.
- Don't talk in volumes.
- Don't smother them with praise.
- Don't make icebergs out of icicles.
- Handle hassles healthily.

3

Percolating Peer Pressure

REMEMBER THOSE OLD COFFEEMAKERS? The kind that existed before it took fifty words to order a cup of coffee? I walked into one of these new coffee shops recently, expecting to spend about sixty-nine cents to get a nice cup of joe. I was met by a young woman who had fifteen earrings—in one ear.

"What can I get you, sir?"

"I'd like a cup of coffee, please."

"Grande, tall, or venti?"

"Excuse me?"

"What *size* would you like?"

"Oh—medium will do."

"Great. I'll order you a grande."

"Grande is medium?"

"It's this size, sir," she said impatiently, holding up a cup.

"Okay. It's just that grande sounds, well, *big.*"

"Would you like a double or single?"

"A double or single *what?*"

"A double or single shot of espresso."

"What's espresso? I thought I was ordering a coffee."

"Espresso is a strong shot of coffee."

"So, I order coffee in my coffee?"

"Okay," she said, not too pleased with my questions, "I'll get you a single. Do you want it skinny?"

"Skinny? I thought I was getting a medium, er, grande."

"Skinny means we use nonfat milk, sir."

"Oh, yeah, that'll be fine."

"I won't even ask you if you want a latte."

"Thank you. I really just want a cup of coffee."

"Fine. That'll be three dollars and sixteen cents."

"*What?* Three dollars and sixteen cents? Are you putting it in a crystal vase or something?"

I'm much more at home with those old coffee percolators that had the little glass bubble on top. You poured in some water, added a couple scoops of Folgers in the metal basket, put the cover on, and you were ready to set the pot on the stove. Soon the liquid began to boil through the stem in the basket, and you could hear the percolating sounds—the promise that the coffee would soon be ready to drink.

Well, very early on, something starts percolating in your children—peer pressure. It can begin as early as grade school.

Parents, how you handle peer pressure—the pressure your children feel as well as the pressure you feel—in the early years will play a significant role in how your children handle peer pressure when they become adolescents. I know a hairdresser who commented on how surprised she is to be doing highlights for girls who are just ten years old. "When I first got started in this business," she told me, "it was unusual to color the hair of girls in high school. Now moms bring in their grade-school daughters!"

"Isn't that bad for their hair, to be chemically treating it when they're still so young?" I asked.

"Of course it is," she admitted. "But they insist that everybody's doing it."

Who's responding to pressure here, the mothers or the daughters? Probably both. It's important for you to recognize how your response to peer pressure affects your children's response. What irritates me as a counselor is when parents cave in to peer pressure and even cultivate it for twelve years—making sure their children have the latest Baby Gap wear, the latest hairstyle, the latest everything—and then suddenly expect their thirteen-year-old to stand against the crowd.

You have the power either to prepare your kids to stand up to peer pressure early on or to turn them into willing dupes who will run along with the herd. In this chapter I want to explore how the early years of parenting will affect how your sons or daughters do when they become adolescents.

For starters, wise parents will teach their kids how to be "different."

Dare to Be Different

Hey, parents. Yeah, you—the ones whose kids have the most fashionable buzz haircut with a ponytail, even though they're just six or seven years old. Do you know what you're really conveying to your kids? You're telling them that they need to grow up to look like everybody else. Now think about what "everybody else" is like, and ask yourself if that is what you really want for your kids.

Unfortunately every generation seems to start a little earlier in the great quest to become just like everybody else. Every season brings a new "must have it" kid craze: Pokemon, Tickle-Me-Elmo, Nintendo 64, Furby, Barbie, Cabbage Patch dolls, Beanie Babies, PlayStation 2.

Apart from a single Furby, you won't find any of the above in the Leman household for a simple reason: I think it's good to be different. I think it's healthy to raise kids to stand apart from the crowd.

If your son isn't "different," his adult life may look like this: He may marry and divorce within the first five years of his adult life. He may drift from partner to partner. If he marries or moves in with a woman who has already been divorced, he will merge his life with someone whom somebody else has already discarded.

If your daughter isn't "different," she may have half a dozen sexual partners before she graduates from college. She may also contract a sexually transmitted disease. Her sexual experience will actually make her less likely to have a successful marriage, leading to a number of broken relationships.

All these divorces and sexual partners will result in yet another set of stepgrandparents and a brood of kids who live in three or four different houses. Your job as a grandparent will become increasingly difficult. Not only will you probably not get to see all your grandkids, but you'll certainly never get to see all of them in one place.

That makes life pretty ugly and very complicated.

I think it's *good* for kids to be different. When the popular route leads to disaster, I want my children to choose a unique path. If I raise my kids to be exactly like everyone else—letting them watch whatever they want to watch, turning a blind eye to premarital sexual activity, running them ragged from morning to night so that the family never bonds, being too tired on Saturday or Sunday morning to take the family to synagogue or church—I should expect them to grow up to be like everyone else.

And that thought terrifies me.

How do you raise kids who expect to be different? It begins with the parents' creating a climate of love, acceptance, trust, affirmation, and positive expectations. My kids know I love them, but they also know I expect the best from them. I hold them accountable and openly share my *positive* expectations for their behavior and attitudes. It makes a difference when parents tell their son, "Honey, we don't expect you to be like everybody else; we expect you to be different." This gives the son the feeling that he's special—and that's a very good feeling.

Instead of trying to make your teenagers "fit into" society's artificial standards, which change with every season, why not put your effort into helping them "fit into" your family, which will always be there for them? Your kids need you to be cheerleaders for them.

Be a Cheerleader

Remember when you were in high school and the cutest girls got to wear those short wool dresses, carry megaphones, and jump up and down on the sidelines?

You know, the cheerleaders.

That's what your children need from you now—not empty praise, but informed encouragement. You can give your children a tremendous gift: Whatever their sport or interest, be an active observer. If they choose basketball, learn enough about the game so that you don't call quarters "innings." If you really want to encourage them knowledgeably, learn to appreciate assists and rebounds as well as making baskets. If they are baseball players, learn enough so that you can compliment them on a sacrifice RBI (run batted in), even though it resulted in an out. If your children are figure skaters, find out the difference between a single lutz and a single axel.

On the other hand, if chess or band gets your daughter going, show an interest there. If your son is into Boy Scouts, admire his badges and sincerely congratulate him on his new awards.

In short, show them you're interested. Show them you care. If you do that, you'll spare them and yourself much agony down the road.

The popular singer Michael W. Smith often says that one of the main things that kept him from going along with the crowd when he was younger was his parents' undying love. Like many boys, Michael had his rebellious days, but he never fell so far that he couldn't find his way back. He knew he was loved and accepted at home, and that helped him tremendously when his closest friends started going to parties and Michael realized he was going to lose touch with them if he didn't follow along. Here's how he describes it in his book *This Is Your Time:*

> In my case, my closest friends started going to all the parties. I knew there was nothing for me there, but my friends wanted me to be a part of that scene simply because they were. Deep inside I knew that if I didn't join them at the parties, there was going to be a change in our friendship, and there was.
>
> Monday-morning conversations were always about the weekend. I could literally feel my friends pulling away, because I couldn't talk with them about the parties. They were "nice" to me, but the "hang thing" was over. I didn't belong anymore. That was hard.[1]

Later in this same book Michael explains one of the reasons he was able to stand against the crowd:

> My parents are definitely role models in my life. The main reason I was able to stand against the partying crowd was because I received the acceptance I needed at home. "Fitting in" still mattered, but I didn't crave it like some others did. I knew my parents loved me, and I respected the way they lived their lives. They stuck with me through the hard times and demonstrated a consistent, unconditional love so that I never strayed so far that I lost my way.[2]

Here's what happens when a boy thinks his mom isn't interested: he becomes unusually peer dependent. If the peer group says that he needs to smoke dope to fit in, he'll smoke dope. If the peer group likes to drink on the weekend and then race their cars down a lonely highway, your peer-dependent son will follow along. If he finds a young woman who thinks he's fascinating, he'll spend all his time with her, and it may not be long before the two of them are quietly whispering about the young woman's missed period.

If adolescents feel that they belong to their families, they have no psychological reason to engage in aberrant behavior! It takes time to be involved in your children's lives, but it eventually takes even more time not to be involved. How many times have I talked to parents who finally start spending time with their daughter—*after* she's gotten pregnant? If you don't offer a home life in which your adolescents know they are loved, appreciated, and cared for, you'll end up spending much more time trying to put out the many fires that follow.

> If adolescents feel that they belong to their families, they have no psychological reason to engage in aberrant behavior!

There's another side to adolescents' need for encouragement. As your children progress through school, the competition to succeed will become more and more intense. Your son is going to graduate from worrying about whether he can hold his own on the basketball court to whether he can get into a good college. Your daughter will move from worrying about having a date for the senior prom to whether she can land the summer internship that will help her get a promising job.

This twilight of childhood can be a scary time. Your children need a place of refuge, acceptance, and belief. They may experience more rejection during the years between sixteen and twenty-five (relationships, school, job refusals) than they will for the rest of their lives. When your son harbors suspicions that his ears will keep him from ever being attractive to girls, he needs parents who hug him and tell him how handsome he is. When he strikes out at bat or struggles in science or just fails to climb above average, he needs strong parents who can look in his eyes and tell him, "Son, we are so proud of you."

The best ways to fight percolating peer pressure are not to give in to your own peer pressure and then to begin creating a sense of belonging and encouragement from the time your children are toddlers. If you wait until adolescence to begin tackling this problem, you're going to make your life much more difficult.

In the next chapter we're going to discuss full-blown peer pressure—and what you can do about it once your children actually reach adolescence. But for starters,

Remember:

- Parents who want their kids to resist adolescent peer pressure must first dare to be different in the way they raise their younger children.
- Kids don't need empty praise, but they do need informed encouragement.
- Children who feel they belong at home won't be so desperate to belong to the wrong peer groups.

4

Planet Peer Pressure

YOU PARENTS OF ADOLESCENTS have no doubt faced the same bewilderment I have when a daughter who once cried at my "cruelty" when I insisted she take a shower every three days begins to take three sixteen-minute showers *a day*. The eight-year-old boy whose hair could go five days without seeing a comb, now as an eighteen-year-old, spends thirty minutes every morning trying to get his hair "just right." In fact, today's teenage male is likely to dye his hair and even use mousse!

This excessive concern with physical appearance is tremendously burdensome for many teenagers because it's during their adolescent years that they encounter all kinds of physical problems: skin blemishes, lack of coordination, and social awkwardness. Just when it matters most, they feel as if they have a tree growing out of their cheeks, sprouting all kinds of zits, blots, and blemishes.

This is all the more distressing to your children because as adolescents they probably want what virtually every adolescent pines for: perfection. Daughters want to look like Cindy Crawford, have the mind of Dr. Laura, the charisma of Katie Couric, and the athleticism of Venus Williams. Sons want to play basketball like Michael Jordan, golf like Tiger Woods, have the humor of Steve Martin, and the likability of Tom Hanks.

If adolescents happen to be physically different—even in the least way—watch out. Things are going to get rough. For starters, they are likely to receive cruel nicknames.

I know this well because my boyhood friends called me Crater-head. I have two chicken-pox scars on my forehead, and one of my "friends" thought that was sort of funny. One evening he branded me Craterhead. Of course, I laughed along with everybody else. Of course, I also cried inside, it hurt so much. To this day I still haven't forgotten it.

Unfortunately I had my own cruel streak. There's a woman I'd love to apologize to. When she was young, she had the flattest chest in the eighth grade—it was practically concave, to be honest—and we gave her a pair of falsies for her thirteenth birthday. Boy, did we all howl when she opened it up in front of everybody at her party; boy, do I flinch when I think about how much we must have hurt this sweet girl.

Another sorry chap in our circle of friends was And-You-Can-Have-Harold. He got his nickname from being one of the leftovers of the choosing-teams process. Each captain would pick a player, and if there was an odd number of people, Harold was always the last person to be picked; hence the And-You-Can-Have-Harold moniker. He was an insignificant throwaway, someone whose presence really didn't count.

To make matters worse for adolescents, Madison Avenue tells them that perfection is possible. Our culture focuses on idealistic images. Even models get airbrushed, meaning that our young girls are literally comparing themselves to computer composites rather than actual human beings. Boys want to be like movie heroes, whose actions bear absolutely no resemblance to reality and are portrayed by stuntmen who have computer-enhanced help. And that witty comeback the hero always has on his lips? Some hack screenwriter probably spent three weeks trying to come up with that perfect line. It was far from spontaneous.

Understanding this pursuit of perfection will help us to unlock what I call "the great secret."

Unlocking the Great Secret

In his book *Preparing for Adolescence,* my good friend and colleague James Dobson refers to the "canyon of inferiority." If there's one thing that characterizes adolescents, it's that feeling of inferiority—that awkward feeling that says, "Nobody else in the world is as ugly as I am, as clumsy as I am, has as many pimples as I do, has a worse batting average than I do. . . . Of course, it doesn't help when the fourteen-year-old male answers the phone and the person on the other end of the line says, 'Hello, young lady, is your mother home?'"

> I believe that self-esteem is probably at an all-time low in adolescents.

Parents are often at a loss about how to handle this. They come into my office and say, "Dr. Leman, just yesterday my little Snooky was so sweet and cooperative and loving. Now she's irritable, cantankerous, volatile, and unpredictable. What happened?" Before most kids reach adolescence, they are well-adjusted, happy, good-natured, and helpful people. But seemingly overnight they turn into something ugly, resentful, moody, and downright disrespectful. What did happen?

The answer can be summed up in three words: feelings of inferiority. I believe that self-esteem is probably at an all-time low in adolescents. When everything in their world seems to be going wrong, when rejection and hostility and ridicule and failure create massive piles of shame, regret, and frustration, many teenagers choose to react by striking out at those nearest to them: their moms, dads, brothers, and sisters. While adolescents may not verbalize it like this, what they're really feeling is, *Okay, life is being tremendously unfair to me. No one in the history of the world has ever had it as difficult as I do, so I have a right to make life miserable for somebody else.*

This canyon of inferiority helps to explain some of the verbal cruelty that goes on between adolescent boys and girls. It's so common for a group of boys to walk up to a girl and say something heartless and mean. Parents should never allow this, but let me tell you what may be going on behind the scenes. The boys are metaphorically thinking, *Kill or be killed.* Their bodies are changing. They've got pimples in all the wrong places. They don't measure up to the older men, and they haven't developed as much as their female classmates. They're terrified that they'll be "found out," shown to be unworthy, unlovable, puny, even pitiful, so they put all their energy into making *others* feel that way.

This phenomenon is why my wife and I worked so hard to teach our son, Kevin, to be different. We taught him that girls would actually respect him more if he treated them with respect and kindness. Kevin learned acceptance by acting with maturity and grace, not by tearing others down.

If kids are left on their own, they'll be pulled aside by what I call the "giant social magnet."

Social Magnet
There is a giant social magnet pulling your children to be like everybody else. What's interesting is that peer pressure seems to be highly evident not only in early adolescence but also in late adolescence. I worked for eleven years on the University of Arizona campus as the assistant dean of students in charge of code of conduct and discipline. My favorite time of the year was in August, registration time. Watching new students come onto a university campus is an experience every parent ought to have. The first few days freshmen can be spotted a mile away. They're the ones wandering around in a stupor, looking up at the tall buildings, bumping into trees, and asking stupid questions like,

"Excuse me, but could you tell me where the TBA building is?" "TBA" means "to be announced." It's a very typical question for a college freshman to ask.

Two weeks later only the most astute of psychologists could pick out the underclassmen. Why? Freshmen have an astonishingly fast learning curve to determine what is expected of them by way of the peer group. I'll tell you one thing—those high school letter jackets disappear, and fast! Many young women go shopping the second or third day of classes and buy an entirely new college wardrobe so that they can fit in.

It's ironic and somewhat comical, but peer pressure is alive and well on every college campus—where students are quick to point out how individualistic and free of family restraints they are. In fact, kids will do just about anything to fit in.

When I was a college sophomore, the ice-cream machine in my dorm malfunctioned and began to give away free ice cream. Word spread like wildfire; all of us had our fill of ice cream (and then some!), with the natural result that the dorm lost a lot of money that evening.

The head residence advisor responded by putting up a sign that read "All of you who participated in the unauthorized ice-cream social the other evening, please put your money in this box because the dorm lost $78."

My roommate and I saw the sign and the money jar as we walked into the dorm. When we noticed that the elderly gentleman who sat at the switchboard—and who was also guarding the jar—had fallen asleep, we looked at each other with the same thought: *Wouldn't it be funny if we ripped off the conscience fund?*

Well, we ripped it off all right, and like most nineteen-year-old kids who do something to be noticed, we had to tell the whole world. We "kept" our secret by throwing an all-expenses-paid party for the guys in our wing.

Of course, it didn't take long for the head residence advisor and then the dean of students to discover that Leman and his cohorts were responsible for ripping off the conscience fund. We had wanted to be noticed—and we were! I was kicked out of school, which was a lot more notice than I had bargained for.

Teenagers of every age long to be noticed, and they will go to great lengths to gather attention. One of the most frightening things for us as parents is the realization of what awesome power the peer group has over our children. Adolescents try desperately to imitate their peers, to accept the moral attitudes and standards of the masses. I remember working with one young man who underwent a 180-degree turnaround in school. He went from an A student to a failing student in a matter of months. When I finally got him to open up, he admitted that this abrupt change in behavior occurred because of the tremendous amount of pressure he felt from his peers to get poor grades in school. He had been an outcast as an A student and simply grew tired of it.

Such behavior apparently has few limits. A disturbing study conducted by Alfred University researchers found that 48 percent of the high-school-age respondents said they had been subjected to hazing as part of their attempt to "fit in." The survey revealed that high school students intent on joining virtually any group— from cheerleading to gangs to athletics, even to church groups— are at risk of being encouraged or forced to take part in illegal or dangerous activities.

For example, these researchers found that 43 percent of the students admitted they had been subjected to "humiliating" activities: forced to eat disgusting things, tattooed, pierced, shaved, or verbally abused. Nearly one fourth of the students reported that hazing involved substance abuse—drinking contests, using illegal drugs, smoking, and the like. Cheerleading teams led this category.

Another 29 percent of the students said they had performed potentially illegal acts—shoplifting, vandalism, hurting someone else.[1]

Paul Houston, executive director of the American Association of School Administrators, told a *USA Today* reporter that hazing occurs far more often than most parents realize because "a lot of it is part of the teenage culture that doesn't get shared with a lot of adults."[2]

Aside from enduring hazing, how else do today's kids try to fit in? Two researchers recently presented to the American Sociological Association a paper based on a survey of 1,796 students from seven colleges. The professors asked students to name five ways males and females could gain prestige at the high schools they attended.

The respondents indicated that the overwhelming way to win popularity was through athletic excellence: 87 percent of males and 82 percent of females listed this as the top way. Grades and intelligence were next: 46 percent for males and 41 percent for females. When asked about the opposite gender, 55 percent of the young men rated physical attractiveness for women as a good way to gain popularity; 48 percent of young women said this for males.[3]

So what do you do if your adolescents aren't coordinated, get average grades, and aren't particularly attractive? Here's the bad news: I've yet to meet a set of parents whose adolescents have *completely* escaped the well-known power of the peer group. Moms and dads of teenagers quickly discover that their children pay much more attention to the opinions and ideas of their schoolmates and friends than they do to what they hear at home.

Young kids today *desperately* want to fit in, belong, and be admired by their peers. You can lessen the pull of the peers, but it's asking too much to try to completely erase it.

Here's how you can begin to stem the tide of peer pressure.

1. Create a Sense of Belonging

So what can you do to guide your children through the canyon of inferiority and away from the giant social magnet? This is the hard part: Just when they seem to be pushing you away, you have to work hard to create a sense of belonging.

There's often an amazing similarity between a twenty-seven-year-old divorced woman and a sixteen-year-old adolescent girl. Frequently they are both vulnerable and very susceptible to being used. And they are both starving for love and affection. In most instances, these desperate traits arise because they had a poor relationship with their father or husband or both, so they go through life looking for some kind of permanent relationship with males, only to come up empty and dry.

When an adolescent girl feels loved and knows she belongs to a family, she won't fall prey so easily to her boyfriend's pleas to "prove" her love by having sex with him. Instead, she'll have the confidence and self-respect to respond, "Well, you're not willing to prove *your* love by waiting until we're married." She won't let a guy use or abuse her because such an action is opposed to her own self-image.

The very best protection you can build for combating peer pressure is to create a sense of belonging in your own family. That will mean putting the brakes on some of your kids' outside activities. If children are always outside the home, you have no way to create a sense of belonging inside the home.

The truth is, teenagers want you to be involved in their lives, *even if they don't seem as if they do.* This might fly in the face of conventional wisdom, but it's true. I've talked to some of the most rebellious adolescents imaginable, and in many cases they were acting the way they were simply to get their parents' attention. If teens couldn't get it by being "good," they'd try to get it by being arrested or getting pregnant. Sadly their ruse often worked. It's not unheard of for a sixteen-year-old girl to get pregnant just because she knows that if she does, her mom and dad will start "taking care of her" again.

If our kids don't have this sense of belonging to the family, they'll find another "family" to belong to—their peer group. Once they attach themselves to this circle, they'll do just about anything to be like everybody else.

2. Encourage Close Friendships

Let's face it. Our kids need peers who like them, respect them, and want to spend time with them. One of the things we as parents can do is reinforce and encourage that one special friendship our sons or daughters might have. With a little help from you, your teenagers will discover a special bond between themselves and a friend, someone who will support them when they are faced with a decision that might go against the group standards.

With the hectic pace of today's activities, it is easy for couples to suddenly discover that they have been parents for fifteen years and literally haven't done a great deal with their children (besides getting them to soccer, ballet, and scouts on time). And

> Teenagers want you to be involved in their lives, *even if they don't seem as if they do.*

then, once the parents get their careers to a point where they *can* spend some time with their adolescents, the teenagers enter a phase where they no longer enjoy doing things with just their parents; the peer group has taken over.

To counteract this, invite the peer group into your home. Make your house a place where your sons and daughters are comfortable hanging out with their friends. Encourage your children to take a friend along on a family weekend.

Yes, this will mean sacrifice on your part. You'll go through a seemingly endless supply of Doritos and beverages. And Dad, you can't walk around the house in your boxers and T-shirt—but the rewards will be worth it.

Help your children build these strategic relationships as soon as possible. For instance, if you notice that your thirteen-year-old daughter enjoys being with another girl she met on the soccer team, make the extra effort by offering to drive over and pick up the friend so that the two girls can spend more time together. Once they have their driver's license, they'll be better able to connect with friends on their own, but wise parents will foster strong, positive, and healthy relationships before their children turn sixteen.

3. Make the Sacrifice

How many hours—or minutes—do you spend with your children on a daily basis? Hint: Reading the paper at breakfast doesn't count. Driving your kids in a car from place to place while the radio is blaring doesn't count either. Neither does sitting in front of a television set. I'm talking about actual time of interaction. Would you be too embarrassed to count this time for a week and see how little it is?

We talk a great deal about the "quality" time we give our kids (as opposed to "quantity" time), but, really, all our kids understand is "time." They just need to be with you, to observe your life day in and day out. Of course this puts a great burden on parents to monitor their own lives. If you want to spend a significant amount of time with your children, something has to give. If you plan to be at church or synagogue three nights a week, volunteer for two or three clubs, play two rounds of golf, join a softball league, or work late, time with your children just isn't going to happen.

That's right. I'm asking you to sacrifice. I'm suggesting that it's a good trade to actually give up something you might enjoy doing during the eighteen years you have your kids at home.

4. Get Extraordinarily Involved in Your Teenagers' Lives

Sally had a seventeen-year-old daughter named Sarah, a very popular cheerleader and homecoming queen. Due to her God-given beauty (inside and outside), Sarah never lacked for dates, but for four months she had been in an exclusive relationship with Greg.

Sally and Sarah talked about everything—and I mean everything. For instance, Sally knows the exact day when Greg French-kissed Sarah for the first time. She also knows what happens during Sarah's dates, what happens with Sarah's friends, and what goes on at school.

One day Greg showed up for a date before Sarah was ready. As Sally sat with Greg in the living room, Greg blurted out, "Mrs. J., what is it with Sarah? How come I'm not getting any?"

In the interest of full disclosure, if any seventeen-year-old boy had said this to me about any of my four daughters, I'd be tempted to heat up his jeans with a blowtorch. He'd "get" more than he bargained for, believe me!

Sally, however, handled the situation much better than I would have. To say she was shocked would be an understatement, but she managed to pull herself together, look Greg in the eye, and say, "You and I have to talk." (As hard as this might seem to believe, this conversation actually took place.)

"When I was seventeen," Sally began, "I hated sauerkraut, despised it. I couldn't stand the smell of it. It made me want to vomit just to think about it. Today I'm forty-one years old, and I love sauerkraut.

"Now, as you know, Sarah and I have a good relationship. We talk about a lot of things. In fact, I know that my daughter is thinking about breaking up with you tonight. The reason is that she is sick and tired of your constant harassing her for sex. You've got to get it through your head, Greg, that my daughter is trying to tell you she is not ready for sex. And I hope I am raising her so that she won't feel ready until the day she is married.

"I know that's how she feels right now. She's telling you plainly and clearly that she doesn't like sauerkraut, and she wants no part of sauerkraut in her life now. And because of your immature attitude toward her feelings, she's ready to quit seeing you, even though she thinks you're a lot of fun to be around."

Greg was shocked that an adult could be so open and honest

with him. His parents had never talked this candidly to him about sex, and he didn't know quite how to take it. But he was obviously hungry for it because a few weeks later he had another talk with Sally.

"Mrs. J.," he said, "here's my problem. A group of guys from the football team corner me after every date, asking me ten questions about how far I got. 'Did you get to first base? second base? third base? hit a home run?'"

Once again Sally restrained her anger and talked very sensibly about the best way for Greg to respond. She helped him to see how wrong it was to use young women to "score points" with his male peers. She also made it *very* clear that Greg would lose Sarah if he tried to use her this way and started talking with his friends about their dates.

When Greg got it straight that he was never going to have premarital sex with Sarah, their relationship turned around 180 degrees. Greg was able to resist the pressure from his peer group because he had found something even better than "joking around" with the guys—a real, even more intimate (in the truest sense of the word) relationship with Sarah. They could enjoy each other's company and have fun together without all the awkwardness, fear, and strain that sexual relations put on a dating couple.

Obviously Sally was extraordinarily involved in Sarah's life, or this couldn't have happened. In most instances like this, young girls will talk to their friends, not their moms. But because Sarah and Sally enjoyed such a strong relationship, Sally was able to have direct input into two adolescent lives.

If I had the authority or the opportunity to give a mother-of-the-year award, it would go to Sally, the mom who resisted the temptation to tear out that young man's spleen and instead sat down to give him some good, wise counsel when he really needed it. Not only did she spare her daughter the angst that inevitably follows premarital sex, but she also changed a young man's outlook on dating young women.

How great it would be if all parents could really talk about everything with their adolescents. Such relationships don't come naturally. It takes hard work, a lot of listening, and a good bit of personal sacrifice. Not only do you have to be there for your children, but you have to develop a gentle enough attitude that they'll want to share with you. You have to painstakingly lay the groundwork for mutual understanding, mutual respect, and unconditional love.

Teens may fall into peer pressure, but I'm convinced that such a fall is usually by default. Remember—Greg came to Sally. I believe adolescents want our input, provided we're the type of people who welcome teens into our lives.

5. Select the Environment

More than ever before, today's parents have far more choices about where their children spend the best hours of their day. When I was growing up, everybody in my neighborhood went to the same public school. Today private schools abound. A few parents are even opting for homeschooling. There are religious-based schools, excellence-in-education schools, and even different tracks within public schools.

Wise parents will give careful thought to the environment in which their children spend between six or seven hours each day. You don't have to "just accept" the teachers your children are assigned or even what group of kids are in their class.

> Wise parents will give careful thought to the environment in which their children spend between six or seven hours each day.

For example, I know one mother whose ten-year-old daughter was being cruelly teased by a group of three girls who teased everybody. When this was brought to the school's attention, the three girls were split up in the next grade, breaking up their little clique.

Part of your job as parents is to create, influence, and shape the environment you want your children to grow up in. I realize it takes time to get to know a school's teachers, to research educational options, and to talk with your children long enough to know what's going on when the teacher's back is turned—but this is what good parenting demands.

Instead of just "signing up" for soccer or baseball, choose a team where the coach is a responsible adult and whose players represent people you want your children to spend time with. Sure, this will take some extra research, but it will be worth it.

I am not suggesting you isolate your kids and try to unrealistically "protect" them from the real world, but I am suggesting that you purposefully present positive role models from whom your children can learn to choose their own friends and influences. All parents are homeschoolers. Parents are the best teachers teenagers will ever have.

6. Provide Stability

Peer pressure pushes hardest when kids are forced to endure radical change in their lives. Stable kids can handle a little bit of peer pressure, but hurting kids, in my experience, inevitably collapse.

Richard was a very good baseball player and a pretty steady kid who never got into any serious trouble. In the course of just a few years, Richard's parents went through a divorce, and Richard's mom moved him from Boston—where he was known and liked—to the Southwest.

Richard's mom had never imagined having to seek "psychological help" for her oldest son, but she came to me when Richard was facing some very serious legal difficulties. Richard had just taken part in an armed robbery and admitted to participating in more than a dozen other home burglaries.

He was only seventeen.

Now, I'm not about to say that if Richard's parents hadn't gone through a divorce, Richard wouldn't have gotten into trouble. I'm not *going* to say it, but I'm tempted to—tempted because this is exactly what came out during Richard's therapy. The most powerful feelings he had inside were the feelings about his mom and dad's divorce. Richard felt that life was being unfair to him and that life basically had kicked him in the teeth. Therefore, he reasoned, he had the right to kick back.

The effect of the divorce was magnified by the family's move to the Southwest. Breaking into a new peer group is very difficult for 99 percent of adolescents, and Richard was no exception. He had trouble reestablishing himself in a whole new environment. Although Richard was a very good baseball player, his sport wasn't played until spring, so he couldn't use baseball as a way to initiate friendships. Consequently Richard felt very isolated and lonely.

Isolation and loneliness create an ideal climate for peer pressure to exert its maximum influence, and that's what happened with Richard. He was sitting in class one day when a guy happened to sit next to him. He wasn't the type of guy Richard would have spent time with in Boston, but Richard was so hungry for a friend that he agreed to go to this guy's house after school.

At last! Richard thought. *A friend!*

This "friend" introduced Richard to other friends, and before Richard knew it, he agreed to drive a getaway car for an armed robbery—all to gain acceptance.

"You don't have to hold a gun or anything, Richard. All we're asking is that you drive the car."

When I last had contact with Richard, he was still in jail.

Listen, parents, your adolescent children are extremely susceptible to peer pressure, particularly if you tear their home life apart. Unless it's absolutely essential, don't move them to a new school, away from all their friends. Try to work out your marital problems before you go the "easy" way of getting a divorce. The more change you bring into your children's lives, the more vulnerable they'll become to peer pressure.

7. Become Your Kids' Excuse

Janice raced into the house. "Mom, can I go out riding this afternoon?"

"With whom, dear?" Mom asked.

"Some college boys that we met at the football game last Friday."

"Absolutely not!"

"Aw, Mom."

"No, dear. I haven't met these young men, and you have no business driving around with guys who are in their twenties when you're barely sixteen!"

Janice went out to her friends and said, "Sorry. I can't go. My antediluvian parents want to spoil my life!"

You know what? Inside, Janice was doing cartwheels of joy and relief. She sensed danger in riding in the college boys' car, but she was too embarrassed to admit it. She didn't want to be the spoilsport and was delighted to have her mom play that role.

Although your adolescents probably won't tell you what they tell me in the privacy of the counseling room, I've found that teenagers are often looking to their parents to say no so they can go back to their friends and get off the hook. Many times teenagers don't want to go along with their friends, but at the same time they don't have the courage to stand up to the peer group and tell them, "No, I don't want to do that."

Instead, teenagers go to a parent to ask permission, using their dad or mom as the "fall guy." When the parent says no, the teens are off the hook! Their friends will nod understandingly and sympathetically because they also know what it is like to live with archaic beings who still live in the nineteenth century.

I know this from personal experience. One time I was fast

asleep in my king-sized bed when a hand shook me awake. "Dad, it's Krissy. Can I take the car?"

I opened one eye and glanced at the clock radio. Its glowing orbs told me it was two o'clock in the morning. Although I wasn't quite awake, I was perfectly able to say, "No, you can't take the car. It's two in the morning. Go to bed."

That's all I remembered until morning. At breakfast I said to Krissy, "I'm not positive, but I think you were in my room last night asking me if you could take the car."

Krissy looked up from her cereal and said, "Oh yeah, some of the kids who stayed over last night wanted to go into town for a pizza."

"You know you can't be running around at two o'clock in the morning looking for all-night pizza shops!" I said.

"Of course, Dad. I knew you wouldn't let me go. But I had to come and ask you so you could tell me no and then I could tell them I couldn't and get them off my back."

I thought about this and said, "Any time you need to get off the hook, I'll be happy to oblige." After pausing a moment I added, "But try not to do it at two in the morning, okay?"

This doesn't mean I'm not flexible when the situation warrants such a response. For example, Krissy knows that our family has an ironclad rule that if you're going out and planning to spend the night somewhere, you arrange it before you leave the house. You never bushwhack Dad by calling later in the evening with a "change of plans."

So naturally when Krissy called me at midnight—just a week or so after awakening me at two o'clock in the morning—and asked me if she could spend the night with Becky, I said a quick and firm, "No. You know the rule. And frankly you should be getting yourself home right now."

"But, Dad . . ."

"*What*, Krissy?"

"Well, while Becky and I were driving around in her car, some guys chased us and flashed their lights and scared her pretty bad. She's really shaky, and her mother said that she'd feel better if I spent the night."

"Oh," I said. After a few seconds' pause I added, "Well, now that you've explained things, that's a little different. I guess it will be okay to spend the night this time."

The next morning Krissy was home by seven thirty.

I believe that parents should be firm when confronting peer pressure but also flexible when they need to be. Krissy wasn't caving in to peer pressure; she was being a Good Samaritan, and I needed to support that.

Remember: Adolescence Isn't Terminal!

When I was younger, my best friend's name was Moonhead. As young adolescents, we cruised the village roads in the summertime, anxiously watching for a driver to flip a cigarette butt out of the window of a passing car. We'd run to get the cigarette butt and then take long, slow drags, feeling eight feet high and at least twenty-one years old.

> I believe that parents should be firm when confronting peer pressure but also flexible when they need to be.

Why did we do it? I suppose there are lots of reasons—to create a sense of belonging, to impress our peers, to feel more grown up. As a teenager, I didn't know how harmful cigarette smoking could be, so I smoked until I was twenty-two years old.

I did some terrible things as an adolescent. You've heard only a fraction of the stories so far. But if you were to talk to my mother today and ask her, "Are you proud of your son Kevin?" she'd say, "Oh yes. Very. I wish I had had his books to read when I was raising him!"

I caused a lot of trouble, but I came out okay. I know what I'm saying when I suggest that adolescence isn't terminal, even though it can feel as if it is. Kids will make mistakes, but sometimes they'll learn from those mistakes and move on. You can't expect perfection.

Look at it this way: We can talk about peer pressure among adolescents, but when it comes down to it, we adults cave in quite a bit on our own, don't we? We know it's not healthy to carry around an extra twenty or thirty (or fifty or sixty) pounds–but still, we keep eating and putting off exercise.

My experience with teenagers is that they consciously know that many of the things they do are not really good for them, but they don't have the self-esteem, the self-control, or the self-discipline to reject them. The best thing you can do for your teens is to model these very qualities. If you smoke, drink too much, or sleep around, you'll have little effect when you tell your kids not to do what you do but rather do what you say.

To help your children confront the inevitable pull of peer pressure,

Remember:

- Recognize that the underlying issue is the canyon of inferiority.
- Create a sense of belonging in your home.
- Encourage close friendships.
- Make sacrifices to spend more time with your children.
- Get extraordinarily involved in your teenagers' lives.
- Select the environment your children grow up in.
- Provide stability.
- Become your kids' excuse.

5

The Fairy-Tale Lifestyle

WHEN I WENT IN FOR gallstone surgery, the doctor was required to tell me about all the risks related to the operation. Because the law insists that doctors give very thorough explanations, my face grew ashen as I listened to every possible complication that could arise from what I previously had thought was a minor surgery. After a doctor's visit like that, it would have been easy for me to think that I had celebrated my last Christmas, that my life was soon to come to an end.

In the same spirit of disclosure, I feel compelled as a psychologist to inform you about the risks you will take with your children if your family life should fall apart. I hesitate to bring up this topic so soon in this book, but as you'll see, my philosophy of raising healthy children centers on the home. If your marriage should break up, you've already put your adolescent children at risk.

The Cost
I don't want to be cruel, but I also want to be frank and honest should you at any time in the future begin to pursue a divorce. If you insist on a divorce, at the very least you should honestly face the price your children will be forced to pay.

Admittedly the popular notion argues that fathers can be replaced and therefore divorce isn't a big deal. Pulitzer Prize-winning playwright Wendy Wasserstein publicly announced that she was having a baby alone, explaining that since she has so many male friends, she was convinced that "no child of hers would lack for 'fathers.' "[1]

But let's look at the facts. According to a report issued by the U.S. Department of Health and Human Services, more than 25 percent of American children—17 million in all—don't live with their fathers. In 1996, 42 percent of female-headed households with children were poor, compared with 8 percent of households headed by married parents. Girls without fathers in their lives are 2.5 times more likely to get pregnant and 53 percent more likely to commit suicide. Boys without fathers in their lives are 63 percent more likely to run away and 37 percent more likely to use drugs. Boys and girls together are twice as likely to go to jail and nearly four times more likely to need help for emotional and behavioral problems.[2] An additional study of 22,000 children found that adolescent girls age twelve to seventeen who lived in mother-only families were nearly 50 percent more likely to use illegal drugs, alcohol, or tobacco than girls living with both biological parents.[3]

Traumatized by her own fatherless experience, Jonetta Rose Barras wrote a book about it: *Whatever Happened to Daddy's Little Girl?* By the time Barras was eight years old, three men had vanished from her life, and the results were devastating: "A girl abandoned by the first man in her life forever entertains powerful feelings of being unworthy or incapable of receiving any man's love," Barras writes. "Even when she receives love from another, she is constantly and intensely fearful of losing it. This is the anxiety, the pain, of losing one father. I had had three fathers toss me aside; the cumulative effect was catastrophic."

Barras adds that "if it is true that a father helps to develop his daughter's confidence in herself and in her femininity; that he helps her to shape her style and understanding of male-female bonding; and that he introduces her to the external world, plotting navigational courses for her success, then surely it is an indisputable conclusion that the absence of these lessons can produce a severely wounded and disabled woman."

Barras personally confirms what I have often witnessed in the counseling room. Women who grew up without fathers often deal with feelings of unworthiness; face a great fear (especially the fear of abandonment); sometimes act out their desire for intimacy by becoming sexually promiscuous; and frequently attempt to "overcompensate" for their feelings of inferiority by overachieving at work, all the while underachieving with intimacy. Barras writes that striving for perfection is "the fatherless daughter's way of announcing to the father who left her that it is his loss. We are at the top of our class. We break the glass ceilings. . . . But it is simply a shield, a tool designed to prevent anyone from getting close enough to see the despair."[4]

While we have long known that young women who grow up without a biological father in the home suffer severe emotional consequences, researchers also are discovering some disturbing physical implications.

Early Adolescents: Growing Up Too Fast

David Blankenhorn, president of the Institute for American Values, cites some revealing research that has recently come to the forefront in an article in the *Journal of Personality and Social Psychology*. It states that having a biological father in the home, having an attentive father who demonstrates warmth and love, and living in a home where there is a close relationship between the mother and father actually delays the onset of girls' pubertal development.[5]

Think about this. Girls who live with caring fathers actually enter puberty at a later age. Why is this a good thing? Reaching puberty too soon can result in numerous societal problems, including early sexual experimentation and teenage pregnancy. Blankenhorn goes on to say that, according to an article published in the March/April 2000 issue of *Child Development,* the absence of the biological father *speeds up* a young woman's biological clock.[6]

Although this next conclusion is just a hypothesis, researchers suspect that a father's pheromones (pheromones are "chemical substances secreted by the body that serve as stimuli to others of the same species for one or more behavioral responses") actually slow down a young woman's sexual maturation. A young woman's exposure to adult males who are not related to her (whether the male is her mother's live-in boyfriend or second husband) does the reverse, actually speeding up the maturation process. In the *Child Development* study, the younger the girl was when the unrelated male arrived in her home, the earlier she experienced an onset of puberty.

The researchers writing in the *Journal of Personality and Social Psychology* article explain that "the quality of fathers' investment in the family emerged as the most important feature of the proximal family environment relative to daughters' pubertal timing." Let me apologize for the "psychology speak" and put this in plain words: Out of all the environmental things that can affect a young woman's onset of puberty, a father's involvement in her life ranks number one.

Conversely, a father's lack of interest and involvement can have dire consequences. The researchers found that "early pubertal maturation, risky sexual behavior and early age of first birth are all components of an integrated reproductive strategy that derives, in part, from low paternal investment."

David Blankenhorn concludes, "What explains this finding? For starters, stepfathers or in-house boyfriends are associated with greater levels of stress, dysfunction and interpersonal conflict. . . . While a father's aura slows down a girl's sexual development, the aura of an unrelated male seems to have exactly the opposite effect."

Blankenhorn's summary is classic: "If we want young girls to delay sex and childbearing, having a loving biological father at home is a good idea, while having unrelated men there is not."[7]

Don't kid yourself. Young adolescents are adversely affected when a marriage breaks up and the biological father leaves home. Unfortunately the damage doesn't end there. Older adolescents keep paying the price, as university professor Marvin Olasky discovered.

Late Adolescents Still Paying the Cost

Dr. Marvin Olasky, a professor at the University of Texas and editor of *World* magazine, has a front-row seat from which he views the effects of divorce on late adolescents (first-year college students). He teaches classes that have between 250 and 400 students, and the papers he reads would break the hardest heart.

Here's one sample: "My parents divorced when I was seven. Like most children, I could not understand why something that seemed so horrible was happening to my family. I was the typical 'daddy's girl' and had a very difficult time dealing with the fact that my father no longer lived with my mother, sister, brother, and me."

The student continued, telling her professor just how devastating the divorce was to her lifestyle: "As a result of the divorce, my mother had to go to work, which she had never done while my parents were married. This all took a great toll on me. My mother worked downtown, so she would leave at five o'clock in the morning, taking my younger brother to day care on her way. My sister attended junior high, so she left two hours before I needed to leave. With so much time, my imagination got the better of me. I found myself fearing death. I was terrified of dying while no one was home to help me."

Another young woman talked about how her parents' divorce led to a loss of interest in her faith: "My sisters fought with each other, my mother with my sisters, my sisters with my various stepfathers, and all the while there was me. The youngest of four girls, I would sit quietly in a dark corner and wait until it was all over. I would listen to the yelling at night and secretly cry. . . . I used to go to church a lot as a kid, but I have not been in a long time."

Perhaps the most telling words, however, came from a student whose parents had been married for over twenty-five years. This student believed that coming from a stable, two-parent household, she had led a fairy-tale lifestyle.

Olasky concluded, "It's important to realize that among many students what was weird is now typical, and what was normal is now a fairy tale. . . . Some students at age eighteen or twenty-one already feel that they were born long ago and have been at least partially abandoned. How desperate is their need to be born anew and held close."[8]

I tell parents who are contemplating a divorce to do something that might sound cruel, but it has an amazing effect. I don't actually expect any of them to carry it out—I just want them to think about it.

I say to them, "You really want a divorce? Fine. I want you to go home, place your little girl on your lap, look into her eyes, brush the hair off her face, and tell her straight out that you are not going to be living with her anymore. If you can do that, you're ready for a divorce."

No Substitute

Anna came to me when her two adolescents were in a heap of trouble. One of them was pregnant; the other had been a runaway who wound up in jail. "Dr. Leman," Anna pled with me, "how do I straighten these crazy kids out?"

It was hard for me to be patient, knowing that Anna herself was on her third marriage. So often as parents we want to improve and fix our kids' lives, when all the while our own lives are a mess.

Let me be honest with you: The advice in this book works. It has been tested and proven many times over. But it is difficult, if not impossible, to build a solid house on a shaky foundation, even though I see parents trying to do it all the time.

You can provide a great foundation for your children's lives by staying married and working on that marriage so that it becomes a model for your own children to follow. If the marriage does break down, then my advice is that you stay single until your children leave the home. It is not healthy for a young woman—particularly an adolescent—to be asked to live with a grown man who is not related to her. Besides, you can't "replace" a young woman's real father. It's best to wait until she is out of the house, and then you can begin dating again.

> You can provide a great foundation for your children's lives by staying married and working on that marriage so that it becomes a model for your own children to follow.

Adolescence is a rocky time. Kids need a safe harbor as their hormones begin to rage, their insecurity reaches epic proportions, and fear grips their hearts. Such forces assault even the healthiest of adolescents; imagine what it must be like to face such hurdles when your home life resembles the chaos of a hurricane rather than the still waters of a protected harbor.

I want to help you help your kids—but the first place to start is with your own life, your own marriage, and your own character.

Remember:

- Divorce actually speeds up a young woman's onset of puberty.
- The painful effects of divorce are still felt even by late adolescents.
- Adolescents, in particular, need a stable home environment.

6

The Great Transfer

I'M A PASSIONATE FOLLOWER of very few movies (*The Three Amigos* is the best there ever was or ever will be—why watch something else?), and I don't watch much television. That means I have to read newspapers to keep up with "popular culture."

One article shocked me with its account of how actress Sarah Jessica Parker was practically mobbed outside a Manhattan restaurant by an adoring band of teenage girls. Parker had been eating with her husband, the actor Matthew Broderick, and her appearance (a size 0 dress and distinct corkscrew curls) doesn't lend itself very well to a disguise.

Even so, these girls, who looked as if they were two winters too young to get a driver's license, came up behind Parker and gushed, "We love your show!"

Even Parker was disturbed by the attention. She turned to her husband and said, "Matthew, they're too young to watch *Sex and the City.*"

Indeed they are! HBO's *Sex and the City* is by any measure a decidedly "adult" series. Parker plays a character known as Carrie Bradshaw, who writes a sex column for a New York paper, touching on subjects such as fake orgasms, the joys of vibrators, foot fetishes, voyeurism, and the like. Sadly these are the subjects that captivated the fourteen-year-olds who swamped Parker.

In spite of the fact that *Sex and the City* serves up adult fare, apparently quite a few young adolescents are sitting down at its table. According to Kate Betts, editor in chief of *Harper's Bazaar*, Parker and her sidekicks now define fashion for the younger set. "They've become a new fashion authority. The clothes on the show are so sexy, and fashion hasn't been so sexy in a long time. The short skirts, the cocktail look. It's in-your-face and fun."[1]

When Parker wore a signature gold ID necklace on one episode, hundreds of teenage girls rushed a shop in Greenwich Village to order identical ones.

When coming across such news items, more and more teachers, religious leaders, and political authorities rail against HBO, Hollywood, and the media for polluting the airwaves. More power to them. But when I read such accounts, slamming Hollywood isn't the first thing that comes to my mind.

I want to know where the parents are.

Have we really given up on our kids to the point where we'll let them watch anything they want, go anywhere they want, and wear anything they want? One study found that nearly half of children ages eight to seventeen say they have no rules governing their TV or Internet use—and two-thirds of kids this age have televisions in their rooms.[2]

If we want to influence our children in a positive way and pass on the values we hold dear, we must become more important to them, quite frankly, than a fictional sex columnist.

In a fascinating report entitled *Sex without Strings, Relationships without Rings: Today's Young Singles Talk about Marriage and Dating,* researchers David Popenoe and Barbara Dafoe Whitehead write, "Contrary to the popular notion that the media is chiefly responsible for young people's attitudes about mating and marriage, available evidence strongly suggests that young people get many of their ideas and models of marriage from parents and the parental generation. The noncollege men and women in our study consistently mentioned family influences as the source of both hopes and fears about future marriage. Yet, according to the participants in our study, many parents have had almost nothing good to say about marriage, and often say nothing at all. Much of this negativism may be due to the parental generation's own marital problems and failures."[3]

Time after time in my counseling room I hear parents pleading with their kids–not using these words, mind you, but conveying the message all the same–"Don't do what I do. Do what I say."

Sorry, Mom. Sorry, Dad. It won't work that way.

Throughout this book you'll hear me stress parenting tools that I have been talking about (literally) for decades–but they are even more true today than when I first started speaking publicly in the seventies. In today's world parents still set the agenda for their kids largely by how they live their own lives in front of them.

> We must model what we teach, or what we teach won't take hold.

Ultimately we must model what we teach, or what we teach won't take hold. We might be able to fool a toddler, but adolescents have a particularly keen nose for hypocrisy and double standards.

When it comes to adolescents and values, apparently there is a lot of work to be done.

What You Do

The Josephson Institute of Ethics has tracked the morals of high school students in biennial surveys for nearly a decade now, and the news isn't good. A nationwide survey of 8,600 high school students found that 71 percent admit cheating on an exam in the past year, and 92 percent lied to their parents at least once within that same time frame.[4]

This means that unless your children are extraordinary, they have cheated at school and lied to you in the previous twelve months.

Now before you get on your self-righteous soapbox, allow me to tell you a true story. I know a guy who is normally solid through and through. He's a Promise Keeper and truly loves God, but like all of us, he can make mistakes.

This guy lives in Oregon, and when his son came home from college, father and son decided to go down to the Klamath River in California and do some fishing.

"We won't bother with licenses," the dad said. "We're going out only for an afternoon."

Father and son drove across the border, parked by the river, and set up their fishing stations, the son downstream and out of sight. After thirty minutes or so, the dad heard some rustling in the bushes and looked up to see a game warden popping his head out of the bush.

"Is that your car up there with the Oregon license plates?" the warden asked.

The dad could see where this was going—as an Oregon resident, he needed a California fishing license, which he didn't have. So he made up a quick lie.

"No. That's my son's car. He's visiting me, and I'm just using his car. He goes to school out of state."

The warden looked at this guy, fishing in his Promise Keeper's hat, and paused. Finally he replied, "That's interesting. I just talked to your son downstream, and he had a different story."

The PK dad was caught, chagrined, embarrassed, and ashamed.

"You know what?" he confessed. "I lied. We knew we were gonna fish for no more than a couple of hours, and I didn't want the hassle of getting a license just for that, so we decided to come out here and take our chances."

While teenagers sometimes seem to ignore what parents *say*, they carefully observe what parents *do*. This dad was a conscientious enough man to attend conferences inspiring him to become a "man of integrity," yet he knowingly led his son into evading a law.

Passing on values is a visual transfer as much as it is a verbal one. Wise parents open their lives—not just their mouths—in order to communicate with their teenagers. Although this may seem way too "passive" for some of you, it is one of the most important pieces of advice I could give you.

God Talk: It's What You Do More Than What You Say

Purdue University conducted a very interesting study on how adolescents develop their religious beliefs.[5] This is what I call "the great transfer": How do you most effectively communicate to your adolescents the things you value most? While the Purdue study focuses mainly on practicing Christians, the findings are relevant for all religious beliefs.

Of those students participating in the study, just over half read the Bible on an almost daily basis, while nearly three-fourths said they regularly seek God's guidance. Clearly some significant transfer of values had taken place with these students, but how?

There was certainly some talking: 53 percent agreed with the statement that their fathers had taught them to pray (67 percent said their mothers had done likewise); 66 percent said that their fathers talked to them about religious beliefs (nearly identical for moms); and 93 to 95 percent said they were encouraged (and taken) by one or both of their parents to regularly attend church.

But there was more than talk; there was also modeling. Researchers discovered three points of transference of spiritual values: kids having discussions with their parents, kids participating in joint activities with their parents, and kids observing what their parents did. Notice, two out of the three refer to actions, not words. In short, your adolescents are watching you twice as much as they are listening to you!

Talking is important, don't get me wrong, but so is the way the talk is conducted. A reasoned approach rather than a dogmatic one seemed to work well with many of these kids. One young woman explained that her father told her "the things he believed, why he believed them, what the opposite belief is, and why he didn't believe that."

Another student pointed out that "I would see [my mom's] beliefs and values in the way she acted." What helped most was when the parents explained why they acted the way they did. One teen said, "[My dad] explain[ed] to me why he did something or why he acted a certain way in a situation."[6]

This demonstrates purposeful parenting: *joining words and actions in a woven garment.* The researchers explain, "Parents explained their beliefs to their children, discussed what they were learning in their own reading of the Bible, and shared what they 'took away' from church services. Parents engaged in various faith-building activities with their children. In addition to taking their children to church, parents prayed with their children, took them along when they were doing volunteer work at church, and told the children Bible stories before they went to sleep at night. . . .

"Our data demonstrated that the degree to which parents used multiple approaches to teach their children about their religious beliefs, supervised their children's religious development, wanted their children to embrace their faith, and modeled participation in religious activities was positively related to how accurately young adults understood what their parents believed."[7]

The great transfer is based on the quality of the parent-child relationship (being neither too strict nor too permissive) and is further influenced by the degree to which mother and father agree on an expression of faith. One of the best ways to connect your children with God, then, is to build a positive, warm, and secure relationship with them as a parent. Earnestly seek God yourself, and bring him into your everyday life. Then, as you model this life in God, explain to your kids why you believe what you believe and why you act the way you act.

I always like to say, *"We don't parent teenagers by rules; we parent teenagers by relationships.*" You can't try to turn your home into a Sunday school once a week and lecture children into the faith; faith is something that is caught.

When I talk to my children about spiritual matters, I like to put my faith in a larger perspective. To be honest, we've never had family devotions, but we regularly frame our discussions from the point of view of our faith. Kids pick up your values when they see you tell a cashier that you've been given too much change, or when you take the time to explain to your kids why you're voting for a particular candidate.

> *We don't parent teenagers by rules; we parent teenagers by relationships.*

Along with that, Sande and I provide opportunities for our kids to receive proper religious instruction. All of our kids have gone to summer Christian camps. It was a chance for them to be away from us for a season while also being challenged by other people to strengthen their commitment to God.

This past summer thirteen-year-old Hannah returned from camp and our conversation went like this:

"You seem to have enjoyed yourself, Hannah."

"I did. Camp was great, Dad."

"Are you closer to God now than when you left?"

"Yes, I am."

"That's great to hear."

That was the end of our conversation on the topic. I didn't pester her with probing questions, and she didn't offer. But you know what? I bet that one, two, or three months from now something will come up, and Hannah will say, "You know, when I was at camp last summer, we talked about that. . . ."

Thus will begin another interesting conversation.

I'm often asked what to do if children say, "Mom, Dad, I really don't want to go to church anymore. It's just too boring." Realize that your sons or daughters may be right. Sometimes, church really is the most boring place for sixteen- or seventeen-year-olds. They have a fun Saturday night, but then they have to wake up early, get dressed, and be quiet for an hour and a half. Given the circumstances, some degree of boredom is understandable. On the other hand, all of us need to learn to do things that bore us. There isn't a single job that doesn't have, at times, some tedious elements. I prefer not to change diapers or wipe up vomit, but as a parent, I've had to do those chores anyway. Church or synagogue can provide the opportunity for adolescents to get ready for adulthood.

In general, I would have a conversation that went something like this: "I know that a lot of the kids at church are geeks, and I understand you don't get much out of the pastor's message, but realistically, if you think about it, there are only a few things in life your mom and I ask you to do, and attending church is one of them. We enjoy church very much; we get something out of the pastor's sermons. I realize you don't, but we still want you to be with us. You can daydream or pick your nose or read a book, but I'd consider it a real privilege if you'd make the sacrifice to be with us. We're a family, and that means from time to time—even on a weekly basis—we're going to do some things together that might not be fun but are still important."

I believe in a multifaceted approach to passing on our faith. Sometimes it involves modeling; other times it involves training of one kind or another. The popular Bible verse from Proverbs 22:6 encourages us to "train a child in the way he should go, and when he is old he will not turn from it." I discussed this verse once with my friend Chuck Swindoll, a popular author and speaker, and he told me that the verse actually refers to training children *according to their bent*—that is, in a way that coincides with their unique personality. Rather than following one rigid method of helping our children develop, we are told to respect the differing qualities of our children and introduce them to life and to faith in a way that takes those differences into account.

That's why I believe in this multipronged approach for sharing our faith. Some kids don't want to memorize the Bible—but they may love to listen to Scripture put to music and accidentally memorize it! Other kids will enjoy going to youth group; some will see it as a chore. Recognize that there are many different ways your children can be influenced in your family's faith, and seek to take advantage of any expression that your children have the most interest in.

Besides passing on our religious faith through a variety of approaches, the best way to pass on other values is to "be real." Although initially this may sound simple, it is one of the hardest things for some parents to do.

Be Real

Mia and her sixteen-year-old son, Jason, had been coming to my office for several months. The stakes were high—Mia was a divorced alcoholic, and Jason's circle of friends looked like an ensemble out of *The Rocky Horror Picture Show.* In spite of the challenges facing us, we were making pretty good progress with Jason until the day he got stopped by a police officer, who found an open bottle of wine in Jason's backseat.

We're often hardest on people who commit our own pet sins, so it didn't surprise me when this alcoholic mom responded with all-out rage. She was still visibly upset six days after the incident when they came to see me for their next appointment.

Things were rocky, to say the least, but there was the potential for a great breakthrough when Jason asked Mia a very pointed question: "Didn't you ever drink and drive at the same time?"

Mia shouted, "Of course not!"

This blatant lie almost knocked me over. I instructed Jason to leave us alone for a while and then composed myself long enough to look at Mia and say, "Mia, we have talked about your struggles with alcohol for several months now. I sat here and listened in silence while you told your son a flat-out lie. I need to know what's going on, and why you did that."

"How can you expect me to tell him I've been arrested for drinking and driving several times? That'll just encourage him to go out and do it!"

What a tragic and foolish mistake this mother made. Jason wasn't fooled by his mom's denial; in fact, she simply reinforced an addict's first defense and worst crutch: denial and deceit. Just as bad, she missed a golden opportunity to communicate with Jason at a level she had never reached before. If she had had the courage to admit her mistakes, we could have helped Jason see how foolish it is to drink and drive, with real-life examples. At the very least Mia could have established new feelings of empathy and communication, but her lies threw that option out the window. Mia buried her head in the sand, and Jason buried his head and heart in resentment.

Not surprisingly I made little progress with Jason from that point on. My guess is that by now he has a long DUI list of his own.

The Real You

My point is simple: If you are going to have any kind of communication with your teenagers, you must be willing to share your real self with them, not just the ideal self you would like to have them think you are. If you are going to enter the private world of your teenagers, you must be brave enough to be open and to relate some of the realities and complexities of your own life.

I realize this isn't easy. When your son was three or four years old, he probably thought you were the strongest man in the world or the most perfect mom who ever lived. At about the age of nine or ten, however, this son suddenly realized that you aren't perfect and that, in fact, you might even fall below the curve on an attribute or two.

Are you going to fight this healthy stage of maturation, or will you cooperate with it? You need a little funeral: The ideal self you once were in your children's eyes needs to die so that you can begin to build a new relationship based on an adult understanding that we are all fallible beings who are in process.

Many years ago, when my oldest daughters were still quite young, I pitched on a fast-pitch city recreation league. During the first inning of a game, I was coaching first base when the umpire made an unbelievably poor call on a high pitch. Almost involuntarily I called out, "You're crazy."

The umpire immediately jumped out from behind the plate, took off his mask, walked a few steps toward me, and shouted, "What did you say?"

"I said, 'You're crazy.' "

"You're out of the ball game!"

I retorted, "Well, I'm out of the ball game, but you're still crazy."

The rules call for players to leave not only the field but the entire park when they're thrown out of the ball game. Needless to say, I was embarrassed. It was the first time I had ever been kicked out of a game, and to make matters worse, I had my two daughters with me. They were just getting a good start playing on the swings and slides when I called to them, "Come on, girls, we've got to go home."

They looked at me with astonishment and said, "Home! We just got here. Why are we going home?"

I said, "Come on, get in the car. Hurry!"

They reluctantly went along and began to press me for a reason when we got to the car. Well, I found myself about to lie to my children, tell them some kind of fish story, but I caught myself. I turned to my younger daughter, Krissy, and said, "Krissy, what happens when you talk back to me?"

She looked at me, puzzled, and answered, "We get sent to our rooms?"

I said, "That's right. I just talked back to the umpire, and the umpire sent me to my room."

My children understood that one perfectly. So perfectly, in fact, that the first thing they blurted out as we entered our home several minutes later was, "Mommy, Mommy, guess what? Daddy got kicked out of the ball game and got sent back to his room!"

As difficult as it was to be honest with my girls, I'm so glad I was. It paved the way for a real and meaningful relationship with them as they matured. Adolescence is the time you set the stage for relating to your kids as fellow adults. As one who now has three adult children, I can testify to the joy and fulfillment of this change. It is different from the unconditional adoration and near worship toddlers give to their parents; on the other hand, it is even more meaningful when you receive encouragement from a fellow adult.

I'll never forget a letter that our daughter Krissy sent to me shortly after she got married. She said that her husband, Dennis, always tells her how much she reminds him of me and that she takes that as the highest compliment he could give her. It's one thing to hear a three-year-old say, "You're the best dad in the whole world," but to have a twenty-seven-year-old—one who has seen you at your worst as well as your best—mention her pride in you, well, that's something else entirely.

Trust me on this one: Recognizing your weaknesses and talking with your kids about how you're trying to overcome them will ultimately build your relationship rather than destroy it.

But What If They Become like Me? (You'll Bump Heads a Lot)
One of the top objections I hear when I urge parents to be real with their adolescents goes like this: "I can't admit to my teenagers the things I did back in high school. This will just set a bad example and give them the right to do the same things I did."

Nothing could be further from the truth. In fact, I have news for you, Mom and Dad. The jig was up long ago. Your children have known for years that you are not perfect. Everyone makes mistakes. The key to a family is to have the people who are close to you still love you—warts and all. You build that kind of love when you share your flaws openly with your children. They will not think less of you; on the contrary, they will be much more approachable and willing to listen to what you have to say.

Besides, your kids are going through a time of life when it is *guaranteed* that they are going to be laughed at. Maybe they'll pass gas when it's quiet, and the other kids will catch them and deride them unmercifully. Maybe they'll use a word in the wrong way or their voice will crack or they'll get into an awkward social situation and just fold.

The certainty of their being laughed at for doing dumb things gives you an opportunity to prepare them by sharing how *you* deal with unfortunate circumstances. I mention an infamous incident in one of my other books, *What a Difference a Daddy Makes*. It's so relevant here that I want to repeat it.

"So, kids, get this," I began. They love hearing stories about me meeting celebrities. (I had just completed taping a Geraldo Rivera show.)

"This woman comes up to me and says, 'You are so right, you are exactly right, Doctor!' "

" 'Who *is* this woman?' I asked myself.

" 'Oh, by the way,' she said, 'I'm CeCe, Geraldo's wife. . . . '

"Without even thinking of taking no for an answer, she led me into Geraldo's dressing room."

"Really, Daddy?" one of my daughters asked. "You were actually in his dressing room?"

"That's right," I said, "and then Geraldo came in and wanted to know what I was doing there with his wife!"

They all laughed.

"But her parents were there too. Still, Geraldo was thinking, *I thought we finished with this guy. Why's he hanging around?*"

"What happened next?" my kids wanted to know.

"Then I knocked Geraldo's beer onto the floor."

"No!"

"Yes, I did."

"Really?"

"I'm afraid so. It broke and spilled all over the place."

They laughed so hard I thought they'd need to make an emergency trip to the bathroom. "Really?" they squealed. "You knocked Geraldo's beer to the floor in his dressing room?"

"Darn right I did. It was a Heineken."

For some reason, they thought this was even funnier, and our family had a good laugh.

"I can't believe you knocked over *Geraldo Rivera's* beer," they kept saying.

What was going on here? Middle school and high school–even grade school–kids often live in intense fear of being embarrassed. The worst thing that can happen to them, in many of their minds, is to be laughed at or to do something dumb. This is especially true of daughters. Their fragile psyches can be rocked for weeks over one careless remark uttered in a school cafeteria.

That's why I make it a practice to let my kids know about situations where I look really bad. Here I am, in a celebrity's dressing room, and what does suave Dr. Leman do? He knocks Rivera's beer onto the floor!

What this does is give my kids a more realistic view of life. Unfortunately, most kids view us only in an "ideal" atmosphere. They see us in the controlled home environment, where we rule and rarely make a mistake. We're confident, self-assured, and in charge. That's fine, but how about letting them see us at work (I think take-your-daughter-to-work day is a great idea), where we might be a little less confident and even slightly in fear of our own boss? It might be humbling for you to have your daughters discover that someone else can order their daddy around. On the other hand, it will help them learn to be ordered around by their teacher—and you![8]

Adolescence is a time for you to exchange idealistic, outdated notions for a real relationship with your children. Don't miss out on this wonderful opportunity by trying to be something you're not.

Remember:

- You leave an indelible imprint on your children's lives.
- Parents can still play the primary role in the transfer of values—if they choose to get involved in their kids' lives.
- Kids are watching us twice as much as they are listening to us.
- For the transfer of religious values, a multipronged approach works better than "lecturing" or formal discussion.
- The most important thing you can do to transfer values is to be "real" with your children.

7

Everyday Hassles

GRACE DROPPED OFF HER fifteen-year-old daughter, Angela, in front of the school. Students were clustered in front of the bus stop: some were talking in pairs; several groups had formed; some individuals just seemed to wander about. A few students were carrying band instruments, and quite a number of boys were wearing letter jackets.

Suddenly Grace noticed Angela's lunch lying on the floorboard of the car. Grace jumped out of the car and called out, "Angela! Angela!"

A few of the students turned and stared. Angela wheeled around and shot Grace a withering, disgusted look.

Now what did I do wrong? Grace thought.

Angela didn't just walk up to the car; she *stomped* her way there, her teeth clenched with intensity. "What *is* it?" she demanded.

"Nothing, honey. You just forgot your lunch."

Angela snatched the bag out of Grace's hand and turned back toward the school, shaking her head so that all the kids could see how very much she had to put up with. *Can you believe it? My mother called me back to give me my lunch!*

Grace didn't realize that she had broken an unwritten rule: adolescents never, ever, *ever* want you to make a scene in front of their peers. As you become "seasoned" with teenagers, you learn that there are some things that are best left unsaid.

"But how is telling Angela she forgot her lunch making a scene?" Grace might ask.

Ah, that's the rub. The rules keep changing when our kids become adolescents. The things that make them most sensitive can be extremely difficult to figure out. And it's precisely these types of misunderstandings that can make living with a teen so frustrating.

That's what this chapter is about: learning to deal with the most common, everyday hassles that occur in virtually every teenager's home.

Communication

Adolescents and their annoying communication patterns (that blow you off with a grunt answer such as "fine," "nothing," "okay," "it was all right," "whatever") probably evoke more parental questions than just about anything else. You want to be a good parent; you want to be involved in your children's life, to share their pain, their joys, their fears, their frustrations, and yet . . .

And yet you want to strangle them when all they can say in response to your question is, "I dunno."

First of all, as parents, we need to know that we often set up a faulty paradigm of communication from the time our children are still scooting their diapered bottoms across the kitchen floor. What is that paradigm? Parents do all the questioning, and kids do all the answering. In fact, we act as if it's an act of rebellion if children dare to question us!

That faulty paradigm will inevitably come back to haunt you. The time will come when your kids decide to stop playing the game.

So what's a parent to do?

My answer might surprise you, but keep in mind that the key here is to understand that your children have a need for you to affirm them, love them, and approve of them. This is more than just a desire; it's a psychological need. If you can become confident of this fact, you'll be better equipped to sidestep the grunts.

The best way to get your children to talk to you is by making sure you don't ask them questions. Just stop, cold turkey! Resolve that you won't ask them anything for the next week or two. Do it suddenly, completely, and consistently, and I guarantee your children will sit up and take notice. They might even ask you if anything is wrong. If that's the case, a good response is, "What could be wrong? Life is beautiful."

Yes, this sudden cessation is going to cause stress in your life. Yes, you're going to see how difficult it is for you to talk to your children without asking any questions. Old habits die hard, but it's important that you persevere in order to effectively "set the bait."

Here's the deal. As predictably as B follows after A, if you stop asking your children incessant questions, they will begin to open up on their own and tell you what is going on in their lives. Remember: they *need* to share with you in order to get your affirmation, so the pressure is on their end as much as yours to finally open up.

Psychologically the ball is in your court if you back off from your children and let them approach you. If they say something that piques your interest, it's fine to say, "Gee, that's cool, tell me more about that." That type of response isn't threatening—they brought the subject up, you're just along for the ride.

In case all this sounds too simple and too optimistic, allow me to recount a recent conversation. After I had spoken to the Young Presidents Organization in Los Angeles, a man came up to me and said, "Dr. Leman, I owe you an apology."

He looked vaguely familiar, but I had no idea why.

"For what?" I asked.

"My wife and I heard you speak in New York. We had been having some real problems with our sixteen-year-old son. He was shutting us down, and there was no communication whatsoever. We were really worried and asked you what to do. You gave us an answer so different from what we expected and so seemingly simple that we thought you were just blowing us off."

"I know exactly what I told you," I said. "I suggested that you stop asking your son any questions. Right?"

"Yeah. And I want to shake your hand and thank you personally because we have an entirely new relationship with our son now."

This stuff works!

Busyness

Let's be honest. Late adolescence in particular can be an extremely busy time. Kids who participate in after-school activities may have to leave the house as early as six forty-five in the morning and may not come home until six thirty at night. Quite often, when they finally get home, they're exhausted, ready for dinner and bed and not much else. My advice here might surprise some of you.

At this stage—particularly for juniors and seniors in high school—I believe it's entirely appropriate to give the kids a little more slack and ask the younger ones to do a bit more around the house. The way I look at it, if kids are doing well in school, holding down a part-time job, and participating in an extracurricular activity, they have a full schedule. So often parents become rigid in chore allotment, carefully dividing up the minutes required for each job so that no child does more work than another child.

I have never treated my kids the same. They have always had different workloads, depending on their situation in life. One time one of the older children complained about a break that a younger child received.

"That's not fair!" Holly roared.

"You want me to treat you just like Krissy?" I asked.

"Yes."

"Fine. Tonight you go to bed at eight thirty, just like Krissy."

"But my bedtime is nine o'clock!"

"Not anymore! Not if you want to be treated just like Krissy."

Suddenly Holly wasn't too keen on being treated "just like Krissy."

We have to adjust our children's schedules and responsibilities based on their stage in life. If your kids are legitimately busy, cut them some slack. Start taking out the garbage yourself, and help them get through this transition time in their life. If you've raised them right, this won't spoil them, but it will make the adolescent years go a lot more smoothly.

At times, however, we have to save kids from their own worst tendencies. We may know better than they do what they can handle, and if we notice that Joe always gets particularly surly when he's out three nights in a row, it's our responsibility to withhold permission when he asks to be gone that third night.

"Look, Joe," you might say, "it's been an awfully busy week, and we haven't had much time together as a family. We're all gonna hang out at home tonight, so I'd appreciate it if you'd tell Ryan that you can't make the movie."

"But Daaad . . . "

"Son, listen, let's not go through this. I'm tired, your mother's tired, it's been a busy week, and we're going to hang out here."

Clothes

Mom and Dad, do me and your adolescents a favor. Put this book down and get out your high school yearbook. I want you to see for yourself how silly you looked. Are you a guy wearing David Cassidy hair? If you're older, maybe you're a woman with a bouffant hairdo that could hide a bird's nest.

And those clothes! Yeeech! Can you believe you wore that stuff?

I can't either.

Within this context I want you to reconsider your last few discussions with your adolescents about clothes. I'm all for drawing the line at young girls' dressing like prostitutes—modesty should never go out of style—but there is usually far more leeway for fashion sense than we parents would like to admit.

Parents and adolescents may argue about clothes more than about any other issue. One survey of parents found that the main disagreement parents have over the way their children dress for school is the appropriateness of the garments (40 percent). Of these, 24 percent say the main disagreement is over style issues, while just 20 percent and 15 percent cite disagreements over cost and durability, respectively.[1]

However, it is important to tell our adolescents, especially our daughters, about things they may not know. UCLA did a study about how young men interpreted young women's dress. They showed pictures of girls who were dressed very hip, and the girls had told researchers they dressed that way to be fashionable. A majority of the boys, however, said that women who dressed that way were "looking for it" and "advertising" their sexual availability. In short, there was a great disparity between how young women perceived the way they were dressed and how young men interpreted that dress.

This is where a sensitive mom and dad can impart valuable information. But to be effective, this conversation needs to take place before your daughter gets ready for her date and comes down the stairs dressed in a miniskirt and a plunging neckline. By then, her mind is on the evening, and her dress has been chosen. You're going to inaugurate a first-class brawl when your eyes (and even more frighteningly, the eyes of her boyfriend!) pop out.

I suggest that in a safe time and an appropriate place you dads take your daughter aside and explain to her how quickly boys can become excited and how the mere sight of cleavage can send their hands roaming. Don't assume your daughter knows this. If you haven't told her, she might not.

When parents come into my counseling office complaining about ongoing fights with their adolescents about clothes, I usually suggest something very simple: draw up a budget, divide that up into the seasons (summer, winter, fall, and spring), and four times a year give them the amount you have to spend on clothes. I do suggest that parents go with their teens to the store, particularly with younger adolescents.

When you hand over the money, you're asking them to make some important decisions. Do they want to spend $180 for a single pair of basketball shoes, or would they rather buy a pair of jeans, two shirts, and a sweatshirt for the same amount of money? You can make friendly suggestions: "You do realize, don't you, that you already have seven Chicago Bears T-shirts and that you may need a coat with winter coming up?"

Keep in mind, though, that at sixteen or seventeen, adolescents need to begin making decisions on their own about what they will wear and what style of clothes they're willing to pay for. If they believe that the amount of money you can provide isn't enough, they can get a job and earn more money on their own.

Negativity

Every parent of an adolescent eventually learns to think of the word *lip* in a new way. Unfortunately, giving parents *lip* seems to be a rite of passage among today's young people.

Hey, I call adolescents "the hormone group" for a reason. They do have hormones running wild, they're fighting to establish independence, and they think parents are too controlling. And let's face it. Sometimes, parents, we are a little too slow to let go, a little too quick with the lecture.

If your kids are generally good, but they occasionally give you a bit of lip, you probably don't need to make too big a deal out of it. Today's adolescents are under a tremendous amount of pressure, and all of us are capable of saying things we don't really mean when we feel pressured. With some kids the best response to lip is simply to walk out of the room. When you do that, they may feel guilty and chase you down in order to apologize. If that happens, accept the apology, and consider the matter resolved.

For other adolescents, giving parents lip is a way of life. A couple of years ago *GQ* magazine carried an article by tennis player Andrew Corsello, who had become known for his bad-boy behavior on the court. Corsello wore his behavior proudly, referring to himself as a "smash-mouth tennis punk."

In response to Andrew's article, his mother wrote the following letter:

> *The aggressive tennis player Andrew Corsello writes that he does not "believe in court etiquette" and instead believes in "hollering obscenities and throwing rackets." How little he has learned in the past twenty years!*
>
> *It was just this outrageous behavior that once motivated his mother to march down from the stands onto the court and force eleven-year-old Andy to forfeit the next-to-final game in a tournament championship match he was winning. The young miscreant—at the time ranked second in the state in doubles, seventh in singles—was then instructed to walk home under a ninety-two-degree Denver sun and say, "I was a rude, loud-mouthed a—" every single step of the way.*
>
> *The lesson apparently did not take.*
>
> *Frances S. Corsello*

The magazine gave Andrew Corsello the opportunity to respond, which he was only too glad to do. Andrew wrote: "Your powers are weak, old woman. Now I am the master."[2]

Although admittedly this is an extreme example, one day your children will wake up and begin questioning virtually everything you've ever taught them as well as everything you ask them to do. Respected psychologist Bruce Narramore explains, "It is as if [adolescents'] brains opened up and a scanner signaled, 'Look how childish you have been till now. All your life, parents and teachers have told you what to do and how to think. Do you really believe everything they taught you? Do you want to remain a child forever, or do you want to learn to think for yourself, and grow up and become like your parents and make your own decisions?' "[3]

You need to understand that this questioning of authority and negativity is in part a normal phase of adolescent development. Your kids are "trying out the world" for themselves, breaking out of their shells, trying to find their place in this world.

In fact, such a phase is necessary if your children are ever going to be able to leave your home and start their own lives. I tell young married couples that they can't "cleave" to each other unless they first truly "leave" their parents.

Fortunately, as Dr. Narramore points out, "most teenagers do not jettison their parents' values, go completely off the deep end, or seriously rebel as they reshape their understanding of themselves and others. But nearly all go through a stage in which they have at least a little negativism and test out their ability to take care of themselves, make their own decisions, and select their personal standards. They do this to prove they no longer need to be dependent on you. Once your teenagers have done this, they are free to adopt many of your values and beliefs while mixing in other role models, the teaching of Scripture, and their own unique perspectives."[4]

Of course, your natural question is, "Okay, Leman, but how much negativity is too much?"

Dr. Narramore has put together a list of normal negative characteristics for early and middle adolescents, and I think his list is very helpful:

Normal Negativity
- Increased assertiveness
- More direct expression of their own opinions about clothes, entertainment, politics, and family activities

- Increased "forgetfulness" about chores and family responsibilities
- Complaining about chores and family activities
- "Goofing off" or being silly, especially around friends
- Making decisions parents may disagree with
- Keeping secrets from parents
- Occasional stubbornness
- Periods of a critical or condemning attitude toward parents or other authorities

Of course, any one of these traits can be extremely annoying to most parents; put two or three together, and you understand why adolescence can be such a rocky time! A much smaller percentage of teens begin to exhibit more severe characteristics, which go beyond the "normal, healthy" range.

Inappropriate Negativity
- Chronic irritability and negativism
- Rebellion or defiance
- A "don't care" attitude toward parents and all authorities
- An inability to work cooperatively, even with their peers
- Frequent depressing or raging outbursts
- Prolonged angry withdrawal[5]

These latter symptoms signal that something has gone wrong. Either your children have a poor self-image, resulting from a lack of a sense of belonging to your family, or they are crying out for help. I encourage you to seek out a professional counselor in these instances. The counselor may, upon further diagnosis, say that your children's reactions fall within "normal" boundaries. But even if that happens, an objective voice can offer valuable advice and put you at ease.

By the way, if you decide that your adolescents need to see a counselor, don't plan on just dropping your kids off. When I'm talking to adolescents, I insist on talking with the parents too, and most counselors will follow this same practice. You have to address what is going on within the entire family: communication, affirmation, discipline–the works.

Learning to Drive

Perhaps *the* most stressful event in adolescence comes along when teens are about fifteen or sixteen years of age–when they learn to drive. I never thought I'd survive my oldest daughter's foray into this experience, and apparently Holly had her own doubts. She wrote down the story herself, and I think it's worth sharing here.

As I started off on my adventures of learning how to drive, a newly discovered sense of power along with the knowledge that two terrified parents were accompanying me was a little more than I could handle.

Walking out of the Department of Motor Vehicles, permit in hand, was one of the proudest days of my life. I ran to the car, threw open the door, and took my place behind the wheel as a proud new driver ready to hit the streets of Tucson. My dreams were rudely shattered as my father emitted a shrill cry. Once again, I found myself in the passenger seat.

Finally after two long weeks of cajoling my parents into letting me try my hand at driving, they miraculously agreed to let me drive home from basketball practice. Once again, that overwhelming sense of power came over me as soon as I started up the car. The wheel was in my hands, begging me to use my new authority over it. The speedometer existed for my satisfaction. The light, the radio, the blinker, the horn–all of it was for my glory.

Maybe that "glory" ran to my head.

Speeding down Grant Street in the midst of five o'clock traffic, I soon realized how humiliating driving can be. I fully intended to stop before the red light. Honest. As a matter of fact, I was even slowing down when I heard my mother make an odd gasping noise and my father bellow, *"Holly!"*

I should have been more attentive when the veins started to appear on his neck and his hand grasped the handle on the door, his knuckles growing whiter with every second that passed. As a reflex, my foot pushed a little too hard on the brake, and all of our heads snapped forward for a brief instant in time. After our backs slammed back against the seats, I tried to point out that the important thing was that we stopped before entering the intersection, but my broader perspective was lost on my parents.

My father must not have realized that he was only one foot away from me or surely he would not have been using such a voluminous tone, thus giving me my very first migraine headache. By this time, all common sense had left my head. In my sheer amazement that I could actually miss the bright red light dangling over the car, my foot slipped off the brake, allowing the automobile to slip only a few feet forward. As my foot almost reached the brake, my father shattered my eardrum by screaming, *"Holly Kristine Leman!"* as opposed to the original *"Holly!"* At that very instant, my knee buckled, my foot slammed onto the brake, and our minivan lunged another two feet into the intersection while the wheels remained in a locked position.

I turned to offer my apology, but my father was gone! My first thought was that somehow he had flown through the windshield, but I was wrong. Out of the corner of my eye I saw a man throwing his hands into the air and doing something that resembled an Indian rain dance around our van.

That's just great, I thought. *My father is providing the entertainment for the rush-hour traffic jam.*

I sank into my seat, lower and lower, praying to God above that no one would recognize me, my father, my mother (who by this time had fainted), or our van. That's when I realized that God doesn't always answer our prayers.

Suddenly my door whipped open, and facing me was that same man, only this time his face had a purple tint.

"Out!" he shouted, surely loud enough for all of Tucson to hear.

Having little choice in the matter, I dutifully untangled myself from the seat belt, and with all the courage I could muster I walked around the van, opened the passenger door, and sank back inside. My father, on the other hand, was still screaming *"Out,"* undoubtedly from shock.

He did break out of that shock, and I overcame my embarrassment. I also got over the power surge that came from starting up a car. Learning to drive was a trying time for me and my parents, but I guess that's why it's called a learner's permit.

While my own perspective might differ just a little from Holly's, I do confess to finding this time to be one of the more frightening experiences of my life—but I'm proud of her. She eventually learned to drive, and Sande and I lived to tell the story.

Sidestepping the Problems
One week after Angela forgot her lunch, Grace dropped off her daughter at school once again. This time when Angela climbed out of the car, Grace noticed that Angela's slip was two inches below her skirt. Almost instinctually Grace reached out to beep the car horn to get Angela's attention, but she pulled back her hand, bit her tongue, and decided to say nothing. If she called attention to Angela, even more people would see the slip, and since Angela was walking toward a group of friends, Grace figured one of them would surely warn her.

Grace pulled away from the curb. One more everyday hassle avoided!

Remember:

- One of the best ways to improve communication with your adolescents is to stop asking them questions.
- When your children get legitimately busy, cut them some slack at home and lighten up on their chores.
- Choose your battles carefully when it comes to clothes; don't fight over style, and allow your adolescents to begin making some of their own decisions.
- Expect "normal" negativity to occur; see a counselor if the negativity becomes chronic or excessive.
- If you want to teach your children how to drive, avoid rush hour at all costs.

8

Risky Business

I'VE MET MANY PARENTS who believe they know what's best for their kids and who bring them up accordingly, with a strict, authoritarian style. For about eight or nine years, this parenting seems to work perfectly. They say "jump," and their son asks "how high?" They tell their daughter to curtsy, and she does it on cue. These parents often take particular delight in showing off their kids, and they beam with satisfaction when somebody compliments their well-behaved brood.

During their kids' adolescence, however, such a parenting style inevitably begins to fall apart. At this point the parents become mystified. They end up in my office and tell me, "We don't understand what's wrong with our kids! They used to be such compliant kids, doing everything we asked them, and now they won't even listen to us!"

You know what mistake these parents made? They always thought of their kids as very obedient, when, in fact, they raised kids who were easily controlled. They probably patted each other on the back many times when the kids were preadolescents, saying, "We've got great kids, don't we? Whatever we ask them to do, they do!"

If you've shaped kids who are easily controlled, what happens when those kids grow up, feel the effects of their own hormones, and interact with their peers? You think they stop being easily controlled? Not on your life. As soon as your children become teenagers, you better get ready for some risky business. Their peer group can't wait to sink their teeth into the adolescents who have been easily controlled while growing up.

Parenting on the Edge

Some of you parents are going to really dislike what I have to say in this chapter. All I'm asking is that you hear me out.

Seventeen-year-old Ginny was a beautiful young woman, inside and out, and stood apart, by her own admission, as the only virgin on her high school cheerleading team. Her blonde hair and blue eyes complemented an athletic figure and an outgoing personality. To top it all off, she served as a student body officer.

Although Ginny was a virgin, she never lacked for male attention. Everyone liked her, and the boys fell at her feet. But Ginny stuck to her values.

Not surprisingly Ginny was blessed with a very close relationship with her mom. They talked about everything. Instead of just waiting up for Ginny to get home from an evening out and then going to bed, Ginny's mom engaged her daughter in long conversations, talking about everything from that evening's date to some of the more debatable issues of our society. Mother and daughter sometimes stayed up talking until two o'clock in the morning.

One Friday afternoon Ginny came home and told her mother that she wanted to go to a party that everybody was going to, by far the biggest party of the school year. Because of their open relationship, Ginny told her mom that she was a little concerned because she knew people would probably be smoking and drinking, and possibly smoking pot as well. But she still wanted to go to the party very much.

It would have been so easy for Ginny's mom to be offended, angry, and hostile: "You're not going to any party, young lady, where there will be people smoking pot, drinking, and who knows what! You're going to stay home!"

But she didn't. She did a very brave thing and told Ginny it was her decision. In fact, if Ginny decided to go, her mom said she would drop her off.

Ginny carefully weighed the pluses and minuses of the situation and informed her mom that she still wanted to go. Her mom was understandably concerned but made another wise decision. She dropped Ginny off at the party, but before Ginny got out, she said, "Ginny, I'm going to be down the street about half a block, where I'll wait for fifteen minutes. If things are not what you think they should be, feel free to come on out, and I'll give you a ride home."

The mom watched her daughter walk toward the house with mixed emotions. Anxiety almost ate up Ginny's mom, and she sent more than a few prayers hurtling toward heaven. Ten minutes later she breathed a huge sigh of relief when Ginny climbed back into the car.

"Mom, it was a zoo!" Ginny exclaimed. "I couldn't handle it. No way! There were a lot of older people there—kids from other high schools and even some college students—drinking and acting crazy. I want to go home."

Some of you may think Ginny's mom acted foolishly. What if Ginny had stayed and gotten into serious trouble after all? But I think Ginny's mom was a brave, wise, and loving woman. She had a close relationship with her daughter and knew Ginny well enough to trust her. It would have been very easy for her to just say no, but she gave her daughter the right to make the decision about the party. She had brought up Ginny in a home where Ginny learned, from the very beginning, how to make wise choices. Although Ginny faced a more sophisticated choice than she had ever made before, she had plenty of practice in making decisions. Consequently when the time of testing came, she passed with flying colors.

In fact, Ginny was very prepared when she went away to college. From my time working on a university campus, I'm all too familiar with young people who never made their own decisions—and then proceeded to overindulge in parties as soon as college provided their first taste of freedom. They simply didn't know how to make wise decisions when their parents weren't making them on their behalf.

Now, let me tell you about another true story—this one a tragedy—about a boy who wasn't taught how to make wise decisions.

Drinking and Driving

A friend of mine, retired NBA player Jay Carty, often recounts a true story when he talks to teens about making wise choices. In the Midwest one evening some friends invited a young man, whom we'll call Scott, to go out driving with them. Elated that these older boys thought of him as "one of them," Scott eagerly accepted their offer and was soon sitting in the backseat of a car.

No sooner had they driven away from Scott's house than they pulled out some beer and urged Scott to drink along with them. Had Scott been told, "Let's go out driving and drinking," he would have said no. But faced with the decision, he wanted to belong. He had never tasted beer before, but this night he decided to go along with the other guys.

About a mile down the road, the driver pulled out a little bottle of pills. Again, if Scott's friends had told him, "We're going to drink, drive, and take drugs," he would have stayed home. But here he was, and he didn't want to look like a sissy, so Scott swallowed the pills.

Then they passed the marijuana. He had never smoked pot before, but could pot be any worse than the pill he just swallowed?

Scott smoked the joint.

Now, drugged up, drunk, and feeling happy, the boys—all football players—wanted some more physical fun, so they cruised lover's lane and found a couple in a parked car. Three of the boys jumped out of the car and silently stole up to the vehicle. At this point, Scott lagged behind. Enough was enough.

Scott's friends started pounding on the car and making a nuisance of themselves, forcing the boy to step out of his car. He was no match for the three football players. They hit him, hit him again, then hit him some more until he stopped moving.

> Children and adolescents must be given plenty of opportunities to decide for them-selves, *especially while they are still open to early parental guidance.*

Now the boys had a helpless girl in their grasp. They put a bag over her head and had their way with her. At first Scott wanted nothing to do with this. If his friends had said, "Hey Scott, let's go get drunk and high, beat up a guy, and rape his girlfriend," Scott would have stayed home. But he had already made several bad decisions that night, so when his friends insisted he join in, Scott took his turn with the girl.

By this time the girl was understandably frantic over her ordeal. She flailed and fought with an increased ferocity, and just as Scott pulled away, the bag came off the girl's head.

To his horror, Scott realized he had just raped his sister.[1]

Parental Guidance and Freedom to Fail

I said early in this book that you can guide your kids, but at this age you can't control them. Once Scott left his parents' house, he was dependent on his own ability to say no, an ability that was sadly and tragically lacking.

Children and adolescents must be given plenty of opportunities to decide for themselves, *especially while they are still open to early parental guidance.* I once frustrated one of my adolescent daughters when she insisted I give her an exact time to be home.

She was ninety miles away at a basketball game, and the team had decided to go out for pizza. But something had delayed them. She wanted to know what time I wanted her to come home, given the new circumstances. I was asleep when the phone woke me up. Our conversation that night went something like this:

"Hello."

"Dad, Dad?" a voice called out. Immediately I recognized Krissy on the other end.

"Who is this?" I asked.

"Daaad."

"Hi, Krissy."

"I just called to ask what time I need to be home tonight."

"Honey, what time is it now?"

"It's quarter to twelve."

"Fine. Just be home at a reasonable hour, okay?"

"Dad, would you please give me a specific time I need to be home? We're at a pizza place, and the football team hasn't even arrived yet."

"Krissy, just be home at a reasonable hour."

"Dad, please just give me—"

Click.

I hung up on her and went back to sleep.

Forty minutes later the phone rang again, waking me up from my sleep for the second time in less than an hour.

I was less than pleased when the familiar, "Dad, Dad?" came over the phone line.

"Who is this?" I growled.

"Daaad."

"Now what, Krissy?"

"Would you just tell me what time I need to be home?"

"Honey, we've already had this conversation, and I've given

you my answer. Be home at a reasonable hour." I then hung up the phone before she could argue.

Krissy was home about one o'clock, very reasonable considering the circumstances. I know she got home at that hour because I heard the garage door open. In spite of the fact that I had been asleep and a little cavalier with Krissy, parents of adolescents can relate when I confess that you never *really* go into a deep sleep until all the young ones are safely at home.

I realize a number of "experts" might disagree with what I did, insisting that I should have given Krissy a firm time, followed by an ultimatum: "Be home at one o'clock if you ever hope to leave the house again on a Friday night!" It's my belief, however, that if a child is old enough to drive a car, she's old enough to figure out what time to be home.

I know some parents might counter, "If I told my daughter to just be home at a reasonable hour, she'd stagger into the house at four fifteen in the morning." Well, if Krissy had done that, it would have been the last time she had the car in the evening.

> If you've never given your kids the freedom to fail, you haven't equipped them with the freedom to succeed.

Sometimes it can be a painful process for sons and daughters to begin making their own decisions, but mothers or fathers who overparent don't give their kids an opportunity to develop their own inner resources.

Most parents today, I feel, have done a tragically beautiful job of snowplowing the roads for their kids. What I mean is, we think we know what's best for our kids, and because we know what's best for them, we haven't given them enough decision-making opportunities. Thus, when they are cast into situations where they must make life-changing decisions, they're ill equipped because they've never been stretched in that area.

Let me be blunt: If you've never given your kids the freedom to fail, you haven't equipped them with the freedom to succeed. In fact, you've virtually guaranteed that they are going to fail.

When I mention this in a seminar, I know some guy is going to hold up his hand in protest. "Now just a minute!" he'll say. "You've gone far enough. My wife and I know what's best for our kids. And in our home we have rules and regulations, and everyone must follow those rules and regulations regardless of how they feel. I don't care whether they're two or ten or twenty. If they live under my roof, they live under my rules. And that's that."

After I've given the man the opportunity to speak his mind, I usually respond, "That's fine. But what I'm trying to point out is that if you don't give your kids some freedom to make their own choices, you are setting them up for all kinds of problems. And when they face the most important decisions of their lives, they may have a problem making the right choices."

Remember, Ginny was seventeen, a senior in high school when she was invited to a big party. In just a few months she was going to live away from home while she attended college. Her mom knew it was time for Ginny to put her training to the test, and Ginny passed.

I guess what I'm getting at is this: Parenting an adolescent is risky business. Some parents fear any kind of risk; they hate the fact that they can't absolutely control their kids' lives and decisions, so they remove any possibility that they will ever make a wrong decision.

The result is often tragic, as was the case with Scott. The question is not *whether* your kids will face decisions on their own, but *when*. And when they do, will they be equipped to handle them?

Finding the Right Balance

I'm often asked, "Should I monitor the time my teens spend with friends?" You can probably already guess from what I've said previously in this chapter that I'm not a fan of the word *monitor;* that sounds too much like an overcontrolling parent who constantly looks over the shoulders of their kids. I can't say this enough: As your kids progress through adolescence, your parenting style must adapt. Kids are going to fight for a greater degree of independence; if you don't give it to them, they'll take it! They are going to want to hang out with their friends and—this is the scary part—they are going to want to have a major say in who those friends are.

If you've done your job well in pre- and early adolescence, choosing friends shouldn't be too much of a problem. At this point, you just want to hold them accountable to live up to their own standards. You can best keep tabs on what's going on (as much as I hate that word!) by making your home the place where kids come to hang out. Yeah, it'll cost you some money to provide the seemingly endless amounts of soda, pizza, and chips that teens consume; yes, you'll sacrifice some of your privacy to do this, but if your kids are at your home, you'll have a general idea of what's going on.

Of course, all of this is age relevant. For younger adolescents I have a rule that goes against the grain of most parents in our society. Our younger kids almost never do sleepovers at other people's houses. Perhaps my experience as a counselor has made me unusually sensitive here, but the truth is, it's impossible to know what is going on in other people's houses. In my counseling office I've talked to some of the seemingly most respectable families in a town, only to discover that crazy and even perverse things happen behind closed doors.

Parenting is a continuum. As kids grow from age twelve to twenty, we need to loosen up a little bit more every year, a process I call "holding them close, then letting them go." We must learn to say good-bye to our kids a little bit at a time: when they spend the night with their grandparents, go away for a week to camp, and then, ultimately are gone for weeks at a time during the first few years of college.

What works for a thirteen-year-old won't work for a seventeen-year-old, and vice versa. When it comes to raising adolescents, "rules" become outdated almost as soon as they become relevant. Parenting teens is an ongoing, fluid process. Kids in this stage grow up so fast that parenting teens needs to become far more about building relationships than about living by hard-and-fast rules.

Remember:
- Kids who are easily controlled by their parents may be just as easily controlled by their peer group.
- Kids who have never had the freedom to make their own decisions aren't prepared to live in the real world, which requires numerous decisions.
- Parenting adolescents is about finding the right balance between holding our growing kids close and letting them go.

9

Toxic Parents

WE'VE ALL HEARD THEM or seen them. They are hypercritical, always picking at their kids' flaws. They are smothering, controlling every move their kids make. They yell and rage when their children don't get enough game time on the soccer field. They are so driven by their careers that their kids feel neglected. We see these parents everywhere—in the supermarket, at church or synagogue, at the library checkout line. They're doctors, lawyers, stay-at-home moms, and even members of the clergy.

I call them "toxic" parents.

Maybe you know one.

Maybe you are one.

As you read the rest of this chapter, see if you recognize yourself in any of the character traits of toxic parents. If you do, I think I can offer you some help.

1. Constant Criticism

Sheila made a startling discovery about herself just by watching Nicole, her daughter, play with her dolls. At twelve, Nicole was just entering the dawn of adolescence. When her friends weren't around, she still occasionally dressed up her dolls, although she would have been mortified if any of her classmates knew what she was doing.

One day Sheila was going into her daughter's room to hang up some clothes she had just taken out of the dryer. Nicole had one of her dolls in its high chair while she pretended to feed it.

"I told you to eat your breakfast, and you'd better do it right now," Nicole demanded. She had such a serious, threatening edge to her voice that Sheila just had to laugh.

But she stopped laughing when Nicole kept berating her doll: "You're just a naughty girl! You better watch out or you're going to get it! If you keep crying, I'll give you something to really cry about!"

How did Nicole get such attitudes so early in life? Sheila realized there was only one place her daughter could have picked them up, and that was from her.

Painful tears stung Sheila's eyes as she realized that she had been treating Nicole (her firstborn) and her other children in pretty much the same way Nicole was treating her doll. Sheila had never realized it before, but the truth was that she was passing on the supercritical, faultfinding attitude she had picked up from her own parents. At the moment Nicole was berating her doll, but Sheila was smart enough to realize that if she didn't change her style and methods of parenting, it wouldn't be too many years before Nicole would be dishing out the same sort of treatment to her own daughter.

Sheila also realized that she was treating her husband almost as badly as she was treating her daughter. It was horrible to see herself the way she really was, and she locked herself in her bedroom and cried for nearly an hour. But she also resolved to change, to learn to hold her tongue, and to think before saying anything in anger.

Constant criticism may be one of the most common failings of otherwise well-intentioned parents. It's so easy to think we're trying to "improve" our children when all the while we're literally beating them up verbally. One young woman lamented to Ann Landers, "I am a teenager, a straight-A student and hardworking, and I hold a part-time job. I don't drink, smoke, or do drugs. I try to be a good daughter, but no matter what I do, my father yells at me constantly. I cry myself to sleep most nights because my father makes me feel like such a terrible, stupid person."[1]

I wish I could say this child's experience was unique, but I can't, because it's not. There are hundreds of thousands of relatively good kids who live with a constant barrage of criticism. Sometimes the criticism can be physical more than verbal: mothers literally picking lint off their kids' clothes in front of their friends or straightening their fifteen-year-old daughter's hair. This type of action becomes inappropriate with teenagers; it makes the teen feel very self-conscious and can be extremely embarrassing.

Where does parents' negativity come from? In most cases—as in Sheila's, by the way—I've found that the criticism is continuing a pattern that was established by the previous generation. Sheila had been viciously criticized by her own mother, and even though she resented it, she found she had fallen into the same unhealthy pattern of relating. Sheila's recognition of her weakness was just the beginning. It wasn't enough for her to forgive herself for the way she had acted toward her daughter and resolve not to continue treating Nicole that way. In order to get over the criticism habit, she also had to look at her relationship with her mother and resolve to bring forgiveness into that relationship. If you think you might fall into this category—and many parents do—you need to take a family history.

Generations of Abuse

A friend of mine came to a shocking realization when he took his children to a water theme park one hot July afternoon. Sometime during the middle of the day he took the kids to a concession stand to buy some ice cream. That's when, in his words, "I happened to catch a glimpse of some fat guy in a bathing suit. My first thought was, *Boy, that guy needs to lose some weight,* and then a horrible second thought hit me. I backed up a few paces, and sure enough, what I had seen was my own reflection in the window of the gift shop."

Children of critical parents will often have the same experience—not with their weight, of course, but with a glimpse of a nasty attitude or a condescending spirit. Let me cut through the fog as directly as I know how. If your parents were hypercritical, you have a lot of work to do if you want to avoid destroying your marriage and alienating your children. Don't for a moment think that you have "escaped." You haven't. You must resolve to take a long, honest look at your own attitudes and style of parenting. If you do, you just might see a critical parent who isn't very nice to be around; but if that's what you see, be thankful that you've learned something about yourself and that you can work to change things.

While all of us parents of adolescents are going to be critical at times, we need to draw the line when that criticism becomes harsh, constant, or abusive. A Gallup phone survey found that parents of adolescents were the most likely to be verbally abusive with their children.[2] Our expectations for our kids are often so high, but why must we always express ourselves in such a negative way? Consider, for instance, why teachers write "-3" instead of "97" at the top of a spelling test. Why do some parents act as if getting a B is a capital offense or that second chair in the band is something to be ashamed of? Why can't a girl accept her place as an average gymnast who participates to stay in shape and have fun, without being urged to become the next Mary Lou Retton?

Just because criticism is widespread doesn't mean it's harmless. In fact, Richard Weinberg of the University of Minnesota Institute of Child Development flatly states, "This kind of verbal abuse (cursing out teens, calling them belittling names, threatening to kick them out of the house) is as bad as a smack in the face, maybe worse. . . . The name-calling concerns me a lot because there's no way kids can feel good about themselves if they hear this."[3]

The Gallup phone survey found that parents frequently called their adolescents "dumb" or "lazy" or a similar name. About one-third had actually sworn at their kids, and one in five had threatened to kick a teen out of the house.

The worst part about this is that name-calling is not only destructive to the parent-child relationship but also self-perpetuating. As in the case of Sheila, kids who get yelled at are far more likely to resort to the same behavior when they become parents themselves.

Stop the Madness

How do you stop being critical? First, make a decision to major on the majors, and let your kids have a free pass on the minutiae. You will have enough huge hassles when raising teenagers that there's no sense dealing with the minor, relatively meaningless stuff. Besides, constant criticism is an extremely unsuccessful form of communication. If you are always criticizing your children, your children will learn to tune you out, which means they will miss the important corrections as well as the unimportant ones. Save your corrections for when they really matter.

> Constant criticism is an extremely unsuccessful form of communication.

Second, learn to say positive things to your children. Wake up determined to find something positive you can say. If there honestly isn't anything to encourage your children about, then at least say something pleasant, such as, "I hope you have a great day, honey." Learning to overcome a hypercritical attitude is a daily, sometimes hourly, determination.

Third, find something your children can do well, something you can encourage in them.

Many years ago I taught physical education at a center for

behaviorally disturbed children. One of my students was known as Fat Bobby. Bobby was as fat as he was tall; if he had been just an inch shorter, I swear the kid would have been round. He absolutely hated PE because the kids' favorite game to play was "battle ball," which you might know as dodge ball. Two groups line up on opposite ends of the gym and throw rubber balls at each other. If you get hit, you're out; if you catch the ball, the person who threw it is out. You keep playing until one side is all out of players.

Bobby, of course, was always the first kid to go. As soon as I said "Start," he had half a dozen balls careen off his mountainous body. It was humiliating, and I could see that Bobby was absolutely discouraged, so I started thinking of how I could stop the flow of criticism that came his way.

One day in the gym I got an idea. "Okay," I said, "I want everybody on the floor. Lie down against the wall, parallel to it."

All the kids did as they were told; then they looked at me as if they were thinking, *What crazy idea have you come up with now?*

"I want you to roll all the way down to the other end of the gym, touch the wall, and roll back. This is a race, but you have to remain lying down."

As soon as I said "Go," Bobby took off like a human bobsled streaking down Mount Everest. It was the funniest thing I'd ever seen. Bobby extended his arms way above his head and looked a little bit like a root-beer barrel going down a hill. He bounced off the wall marking the halfway point like an Olympic swimmer doing an expert flip-turn and rode his lead all the way to the finish line. It wasn't even close.

Guess what became a ritual in our class?

Finally Bobby had something to take pride in. He was willing to endure all the taunts (this was a special education class, these were not "nice" kids by any stretch of the imagination) as long as he knew the rolling race was coming up. I called him Roller Bobby, which put a big smile on his face and even led him to hug me.

If you find yourself criticizing your children for things they don't do well, find something they excel in, and focus on that. All kids need to know they are good at something—it might be an honor society, drama, speech, music, art, or athletics; the skill itself doesn't matter as much as the fact that your children have something you can be positive about.

Fourth, if there is a generational pattern of criticism in your family history, consider going to a counselor. You may need some help to break out of this trap.

2. Smother Mothers and Hover Dads

Here's a terrifying truth: Your teens can do whatever they want to do. If they want to get drunk with their peers, they can. If they want to smoke dope, they can find a way. If they are absolutely determined to spray-paint houses at midnight, there is very little parents can do to prevent them.

I've seen mothers openmouthed, completely horrified when they realize that their once adorable three-year-old son has suddenly grown up into a young man who is now breaking car windows just for fun and that their precious daughter is capable of stealing two hundred dollars' worth of clothing from the mall.

You can overpower a five-year-old, but you can't ultimately control a twelve-year-old, and certainly not a sixteen-year-old. You can guide children, but the opportunity to actually control children once they reach adolescence is extremely limited.

Your daughter knows that breath mints and careful disposal of the bottles will probably hide her alcohol use. Your son has figured out that he can hide cigarettes and pornography, not to mention condoms, if he really wants to.

As much as this truth scares you, it is essential for you to come to grips with it for this reason: an overprotective parenting style is a prescription for

> An overprotective parenting style is a prescription for disaster.

disaster. You need to find balance. When I hear about teenagers who have been involved in horrible crimes, I often say, "With some authority I can tell you one thing about those kids: either they grew up in a home where their parents gave them far too many things, or they grew up in a very neglectful home. The parents either overdid it or underdid it, one of those extremes."

Smothering indulgence and cruel neglect create the same diseased personalities that lead young people into all kinds of trouble.

One thing that a "smother mother" does for her child is to make excuses. If the girl wants to skip school to attend a Backstreet Boys concert in a faraway town, her mother writes a note. If she forgets to do her one daily chore but has a hot date, the smother mother shrugs her shoulders and lets her go out anyway.

What this does, unfortunately, is create weak and irresponsible children. My kids know that I will die for them, provide for them, protect them, forgive them, and love them, but *I will never make excuses for them or lie for them.* I won't make them weaker by allowing them to avoid personal responsibility.

I've seen too many men "hide" behind their wives to get away with their alcoholism or to provide cover for their parole officer. These "grown" men have learned that covering up for men is what women do. I've seen women who are completely unequipped for marriage, expecting their husbands to bail them out for failing to pay their bills on time because "that's what my daddy always did."

Smother parents also fail to give their children room to fail. In short, they strive for symbol over substance. By that I mean they want the appearance of having successful children, even if their offspring are anything but successful.

A case in point includes school grades. Patrick Welsh, an English teacher at T. C. Williams High School in Alexandria, Virginia, wrote a very interesting article on parental reactions to grades. "Ever more concerned about their child's chances of getting into their version of an elite school, parents have become shameless in lobbying for grades. Not just any grade, either; for many, it has to be an A. I've had kids weeping over grades of B, and parents of mediocre students telling me that anything less than an A is 'unacceptable.'"

Welsh goes on to point out, "Often, parents won't accept the fact that a kid isn't capable of getting an A and blame both the teacher and the child."

What happens next is saddest of all: the parents start to lobby for their kids in a way that actually holds their children back. Guidance counselor Mary McCarthy told Welsh, "Kids have to start learning to advocate for themselves. Parents take that away from them when they are constantly calling the school and intervening."[4]

In other words, parents are more concerned with having kids who *look* like A students rather than kids who are actually developing the intelligence and study habits of A students. What this translates into is that they seek children who learn to *look* like adults without having the emotional maturity of adults.

I dare you. When you are at the school science fair, try to pick out the projects that are done by the students themselves.

This parental intervention and pressure carries on even into college. John Blackburn has been dean of admissions at the University of Virginia since 1985, and one of his biggest beefs during interviews is when parents do more talking than the kids! "I get the sense that they would like to take the interview for their kids. They say, '*We* are going to the university.'"[5]

Wise students recognize what's going on. Welsh quotes a very mature-sounding college senior, Anna Gabbert, who told him, "When you go to college, you aren't going to have your mother looking over your shoulder, smothering you. If you haven't formed good study habits in high school on your own . . . if you are working only because your parents are threatening you, how can you do well in college?"[6]

Part of being a good parent to adolescents is recognizing your limitations. It's time to stop smothering and to build responsible children who are self-motivated.

Dads can become "hover dads" when they refuse to offer a little more distance as their daughters begin to develop. That cuddly little eight-year-old may not feel quite so comfortable sitting in your lap and giving you a kiss when she's a fourteen-year-old. Don't take this personally, Dad. Just back off, and let her go. When she wants a hug, be generous with your affection, but don't force it. Her desire to develop some independence is natural and healthy, and you need to respect it.

You're going to have to get to know your children well enough to figure out what's appropriate here because the rules will constantly change. Mom, does your son want you to hug him and kiss him in front of his friends, or would he prefer you just give him a simple wave? Dad, does your daughter want your quick kiss on the lips to become a peck on the cheek or forehead? Look for clues. Don't be afraid to talk outright to your children about it.

Ultimately it's all about respect. Your children are growing up and deserve to be treated accordingly.

One of the biggest dangers of smothering is when the situation backfires. Kelly, age fifteen, is such a case. She came to me at the suggestion of her parents, who were concerned about the changes they were seeing in Kelly's life. Kelly's mom was a home economics teacher, a perfectionistic, high-strung woman, and very overprotective of Kelly. As president of the PTA, Kelly's mom had very strong ideas about parenting and very definite ideas about Kelly, the youngest of her three children.

Kelly's dad was an easygoing, laid-back dentist with a very heavy workload. He kept his emotions to himself, often checked out of life at home, and was enjoying the serenity of a near empty-nest home. (The older two children were both in college.)

And then Kelly hit adolescence, and when she hit it, she hit it *hard.*

"My whole life has been mapped out by my mom," Kelly told me. "She knows exactly what I should do for a vocation, exactly what I should study, the type of guy I should date, and what type of clothes I should wear. But I'm not a child anymore, and I'd like a little input!"

When I talked to Kelly's parents, I got the other side of the picture: "We're very worried about Kelly," her mom confessed. "She's bright, outgoing, an excellent student—I'll give her that. But she is also lazy, self-centered, and manipulative. She's also started cutting classes at school."

At age fourteen, Kelly showed an inordinate desire to date older guys. Her parents, understandably, initially resisted but finally gave in.

Kelly lurched downward as her fifteenth birthday approached. Openly defiant to her parents, she exacerbated the situation by using filthy and insulting language. Mom (remember she's the PTA president) started getting calls from school. Not only was Kelly playing the role of the truant, when she did show up, she was often drunk—including once at her eight-thirty morning class. The final straw that brought Kelly into my office was when school officials caught her in the backseat of a car making out with a nineteen-year-old student.

Within minutes Kelly was defiantly telling me that there was no way her mom was going to control her life and that if I thought I could change that, I was crazy.

"Kelly," I said, "describe your mom for me."

"Controlling. Overprotective. Archaic. Old fashioned. Unrealistic. *Completely* out of touch."

"Anything else?" I inquired.

"Boring," Kelly added. "Booorrrrinnng."

I got the picture.

"I'm the only one of my friends who has a midnight curfew *on the weekends!*" Kelly lamented.

The game Kelly was playing became clear to me. Her life theme was this: "I matter in life only when I'm in control, when I defeat my parents' attempt to rule me, and when I turn the tables and boss them around."

I must confess there were times when I felt helpless due to Kelly's almost fanatical desire to be the opposite of what her mom wanted her to be. Unfortunately her mom didn't help matters much. She wasn't very good at following my advice to back off for a while and give Kelly some room, so Kelly predictably responded by breaking even more rules . . . at great expense to her own well-being.

She defiantly broke curfew, sometimes staying out past midnight just to show that she could. Her parents responded by clamping down even harder, which Kelly met by sneaking out of the house and then finally by running away.

At the tender age of fifteen, Kelly left home for thirteen months. She quit school, lost almost all contact with her former friends, and began to associate with a new group of friends, none of whom had regular employment and all of whom spent about eight hours a day perched on top of motorcycles—every mother's worst fear.

The thirteen months carved their way into Kelly's life in a particularly harsh manner. She was transformed from a relatively naïve and sweet young lady into a hard and abused young woman. During one stretch she moved into a home inhabited by three young men, ages nineteen to twenty-two, who had their way with her sexually and who sometimes brought home their friends "to share" Kelly with. She was used in the truest and cruelest sense of the word. In just over a year she became pregnant twice and had two abortions.

Like the Prodigal Son, Kelly finally woke up one day and realized things had gotten worse. Her cocaine-addicted boyfriend had dumped her as soon as she told him she was pregnant, so she was once again alone and wanted to contact her parents. To make the first overture, she called me. I was speaking to a client at the time, but when my receptionist told me who it was, I took the call anyway. Kelly's parents were worried sick about her, and I didn't know if Kelly would ever call back if I refused the call.

In a weak and trembling voice, the once-defiant adolescent asked me, "Can I see you?"

When Kelly walked into my office that afternoon, my heart sank. The pretty, blonde-haired fifteen-year-old was gone. In her place stood a rough, beaten-down woman, who literally looked used and whose language was littered with profanity. Her eyes were hollow and darting; her inability to look at me as she talked betrayed her lack of self-respect.

"Have you had enough 'freedom'?" I asked Kelly. "Are you ready to go home?"

Kelly cried and shook her head yes.

I called Kelly's parents, and they rushed to my office. The four of us spent the afternoon talking about many of the same issues we had talked about a year earlier: responsibilities, curfews, language, smoking, drinking, drugs, and Kelly's attitudes. We drew up an agreement that everybody committed to live by.

As I watched the newly reunited family leave the office arm-in-arm, I knew it wasn't going to be easy. Kelly would still be tempted to rebel. Her mom would still find it difficult not to be overbearing and overprotective, not to mention feel guilty about what had happened to Kelly. The dad would have his own challenge to come out of his emotional cocoon and involve himself in his daughter's emotional world. It was going to be quite a trial for the three of them to heal a relationship that had been so radically damaged.

Since that day many years ago, I have spent several additional sessions with Kelly. I didn't give her more rules, however. I didn't try to control her. Instead we talked about how special she is and about her need to treat herself as special if she is ever going to be in a position to attract people who are good for her, people who will respect her and who won't abuse her.

Kelly is now living a fairly normal life. She went back to school and began allowing her parents to parent her. She didn't always like it. Home may not have seemed like heaven, but it sure beat the "hell" she had been through.

Soon after Kelly returned home, I asked her, "If you could tell teenagers one thing, what would it be? What would be your personal advice to others your own age and in the same stage of rebellion?"

Kelly offered two things. "First, try to realize that even though your parents seem out of it, they really do love you and care about what happens to you. Second, stick it out at home no matter how bad it is. Living out there in the world by yourself is the pits."

Parents, don't fool yourself into thinking Kelly is an extreme case. She's not. I had many case histories to choose from, many of them as heartrending as this sad tale, with many of the same hurts, trials, tribulations, and with basically the same results. Given time, even the most hard-hearted teenagers usually learn that there isn't a better place on earth than home.

But you can't force them to come back home. You can't force them to stay, to obey your rules, to listen to your advice. How you exert your influence must change as your children become adolescents. Kelly was an angry and resentful young woman who wanted her freedom from a mom who was determined to make all of her decisions for her. Fortunately—for all of them—Kelly came home, and everybody got a second chance. The story doesn't always have this kind of happy ending, however, and certainly most parents would prefer their children learn their lessons with a little less heartache.

Kelly had to learn that she needed her parents. As much as she thought she was an adult, she wasn't, and her poor decisions proved it. Kelly's mom, on the other hand, needed to learn how to love her daughter with open arms. She had to learn— as all of us do—how to walk the tightrope between giving Kelly the love and guidance she needed and giving her enough freedom to grow.

Let's talk about walking this fine line.

Become a Less Controlling Parent

The bottom line is this: You must allow adolescents to have some freedom. I realize you also need order and structure, but even here creative parents will find a way to keep track of their adolescents while not hovering over them.

For example, I know of one set of parents who had sign-out sheets in their kitchen. As stupid as this might sound, it's actually not a bad idea, particularly when both parents work outside the home. If John comes home after school, he jots down a quick message: "Mom, I'm at Michael's house; be back at six o'clock. Remember, I have a band concert tonight at seven-thirty."

What this does is give John a sense of freedom—he is free to visit a friend's house without checking in with his mom as long as he lets his mom and dad know where he is. Should something come up, John's parents know where to reach him, but John doesn't feel tethered to the house just because both parents are at work.

> You must allow adolescents to have some freedom.

Another exercise I like to assign to controlling parents is called "slipping your kid a commercial." This practice involves encouraging your children with positives rather than trying to control them with negatives.

For example, just recently I was driving in the car with soon-to-be fourteen-year-old Hannah, and I started encouraging her with positive statements: "Hannah, I just want you to know I'm really proud of you as I watch you grow up. You're not calling boys every other minute; you enjoy good, clean fun with friends—and by the way, you're making some really good choices about the kinds of friends you hang out with."

Although I am *influencing* Hannah by reinforcing good decisions she is already making, I am not *controlling* her. Encouragement is more subtle, more respectful, and ultimately much more effective.

Finally, rather than try to control your children with words, hold them accountable with reality. I speak a lot about reality discipline in my book *Making Children Mind without Losing Yours,* but let me give just one example here. Let's say your son Gary comes home from high school with a letter that basically says that he hasn't done a lick of schoolwork in more than two weeks. (One telltale sign of being too controlling, by the way, is if your kid is a slob or a procrastinator—both maladies are symptoms of a kid's silent rebellion against feeling controlled.)[7]

If you are controlling parents, you will immediately respond with a hundred and one rules; you will require that Gary show you his homework every morning before he goes to school and probably quiz Gary over what is due the next day as soon as he comes home in the afternoon.

Such controlling is exhausting, for both parent and son, so I have a better solution: Let reality be your son's teacher. If Gary were my child, we would have a conversation something like this:

"Gary, look at this letter your teacher sent to me. I frankly don't understand why it's written to me instead of you, but regardless of that, your teacher is saying you haven't done any of your work over the past several weeks. I don't know what's going on. Anything we need to talk about?"

"Nah, Dad, it's no big deal."

"Well, it sounds like a big deal to the school. Obviously you need some extra time to catch up on your schoolwork, so let me tell you what I'm going to do. I'm calling Coach Wilson tomorrow and telling him you don't have permission to play or practice basketball until your schoolwork gets taken care of."

Next, I would hand Gary a five-by-seven card. "Gary, this is your key to playing basketball. I want it signed by your teachers, saying that you're doing okay in school now and that all your work is current. We'll take it one week at a time. As soon as your teachers say you're caught up, I'll call Coach Wilson and tell him you're eligible to play. I know you don't like history and that you love basketball, but history is just as important."

Notice, I didn't say history is *more* important. This isn't the time for a lecture, and during these tense moments it's best not to provoke your children. Instead, focus on letting your son take accountability for his own actions. If he wants to play basketball, he has to take care of school. It's not your job to monitor Gary's progress on a day-by-day basis. By the time he's in high school, he should be doing that himself.

3. Out-of-Control Sports Parents

In a tragic incident Michael Costin was viciously beaten in front of his two children. Although his two young boys pleaded with the assailant for their dad's life, the perpetrator wouldn't listen. He was angry, and he was going to get his revenge.

Sadly he did. Costin slipped into a coma, from which he never recovered.

What was the fight about?

A Little League hockey game.

Apparently the boys got a little rough out on the ice, and one of the fathers decided to settle matters afterward with Costin, who had been coaching them.

Out-of-control parents at sporting events have become a national concern. The following are just a few incidents collected in a report recently printed in *Sports Illustrated* magazine:

- In April 1999 Ray Knight was charged with simple battery, disorderly conduct, and fighting in a public place after a girls' softball game.
- In October 1999 at least fifty parents and players got into a brawl at the end of a football game involving eleven- to thirteen-year-olds in Swiftwater, Pennsylvania.

- After complaining that his son hadn't improved as a hockey player all season long, an enraged father in Staten Island, New York, attacked the son's coach with two hockey sticks, hitting him in the face and bloodying the coach's nose.
- A disgruntled Little League dad beat up the manager of the opposing team in Sacramento, California, in April 1999.
- A Pennsylvania policeman was convicted of corruption of a minor in August 1999 for paying two dollars to a ten-year-old Little League pitcher to hit a batter with a fastball.
- In September 1999 an Ohio man ran onto a high school soccer field after his fourteen-year-old son got into a tussle with an opposing player. The father hit the other player in the mouth.[8]

Michigan State conducted a survey and found that of the 20 million American kids who participate in organized sports, about 14 million will drop out before age thirteen, mostly because their parents have turned recreational sports into "a joyless, negative experience." One psychologist, who works with troubled young people, asked kids who had gotten into trouble why they had dropped out of sports. "Kid after kid gave the same two reasons: negative coaches and negative parents."

A former swimming coach said that one of the things that finally caused her to give up coaching was what happened one day as a young swimmer was finishing a twenty-five-meter race. The father, fully dressed, jumped down from the stands and into the waist-deep pool, then starting slapping the water right next to his son's face. He began yelling, "You didn't finish hard enough! You let them pass you!" Says the coach, "I still think about going back, but I don't want to deal with the parents. They're trying to live out their fantasies. Some of them think they have the next Mark Spitz."

Even though statistically the odds are extremely small that any child will play any sport professionally, parents put enormous pressure on ten- and eleven-year-old children, fearing that they'll never get a good scholarship if they don't improve, and if they don't get a good scholarship, they won't play at a national college, and if they don't play for a national college, they won't get drafted.

I've got news for you: Your kid probably isn't going to be drafted anyway! And in the process, you've just trashed your kid's values.

Joel Fish, director of the Center for Sports Psychology in Pennsylvania, admits that even seemingly mild-mannered parents can get carried away. "Something deep down inside happens in moms and dads when they see their kid up there with the bases loaded. These are well-intentioned parents. We know the people booing the loudest are pretty straitlaced in their everyday lives. I can't tell you how many times I've heard a parent say: 'Did I really yell at the sixteen-year-old umpire? Did I really yell at my kid?' "

Such actions are really a reverse form of self-image dependency. Frank Smoll, a sports psychologist, points out that in a healthy situation, children derive feelings of self-worth and self-esteem from their parents. All too often this process is being turned on its head because some parents are beginning to overidentify with their athletic adolescents. "So it's not just Johnny or Mary out there," Smoll says. "The *parents* are playing the game out there, maybe trying to live out a past glory or attain some athletic excellence they were denied or incapable of attaining."

William Nack and Lester Munson end their *Sports Illustrated* article with perhaps one of the most telling anecdotes I have ever come across. Alan Goldberg, a psychology consultant for child sports, reports that one time at a swim meet he came across an irate mother who slapped her nine-year-old daughter across the face in front of everyone, screaming, "Don't you ever do that to me again!"

What had the girl done? She had shown up late for her heat and had been disqualified. Know why she showed up late? Goldberg explains, "Her mother never asked. She missed her race because two heats earlier her best friend had had a lousy swim and was devastated, sobbing in the locker room. This girl had been in there comforting her friend."

Sports may have a place in children's development, but do yourself and your kids a favor: keep the results in perspective.

4. Career-Driven Parents

Researchers David Popenoe and Barbara Dafoe Whitehead have discovered in this country what they call a "loss of child centeredness" that may be contributing to children running freely. The statistics really are startling. In the middle of the 1800s more than 75 percent of all households included children under the age of eighteen. "One hundred years later, in 1960, this number had dropped to slightly less than half of all households. Now, just four decades later, only 34 percent of households include children."[9] Think about that—over the last several generations we've gone from almost everybody having children in their home to only one in three.

Think that doesn't make a difference in how people view the importance of raising children?

This lack of child centeredness means that children no longer come first. Yesterday's notions of sacrificing for children seem suddenly out of date. "In a Detroit area sample of women, the proportion of women answering *no* to the question 'Should a couple stay together for the sake of the children?' jumped from 51 percent to 82 percent between 1962 and 1985. A nationally representative sample found only 15 percent of the population agreeing that 'when there are children in the family, parents should stay together even if they don't get along.'"[10]

More and more, children are having to "share" their parents with bosses and vocational responsibilities. Surprisingly some parents think their kids will appreciate them more if they become very successful—even at the expense of family time. On the contrary, the reverse is true: just ask Julian Lennon.

It's hard to imagine anyone having a more fame-filled and wildly successful career than the late great Beatle, John Lennon. But from his personal remarks, it's clear that John's son, Julian, would have preferred a middle-class father who hung out at home a bit more. In fact, having a famous father has been somewhat of a burden for Julian. Sometimes, when he's eating at a restaurant that has a jukebox and someone recognizes him, people will play a Beatles song to, in Julian's words, "see if I'll flinch."

Although Julian appreciates his musical heritage and the genes that his father passed down (Julian makes his living, as his father did, by recording music), he's very clear about the limits of being John's son: "The only thing he taught me was how not to be a father."

Julian's anger is quite evident: "He walked out the bloody door and was never around. . . . I'd admire him on TV—listen to his words and opinions. But for someone who was praised for peace and love and wasn't able to keep that at home, that's hypocrisy."[11]

Let me talk to you ambitious moms and dads out there: You'll never become as famous as John Lennon. Few people will ever reach that level of fame and notoriety, but even if you did, it won't matter nearly as much to your children as will the fact that you love them, are there for them, and have made yourself a part of their lives.

Even so, day after day I come across parents making the poor trade of sacrificing family time on behalf of their jobs. In fact, I know of one junior high mom who actually bragged about her "cleverness" when she got another mom to videotape a swim meet her son was competing in. "I was able to get more work done and still got to see him swim!" she raved. But her son's sullen disposition said it all: a video camera is a poor substitute for a mother's presence.

Some years ago I was asked to speak to a group of military wives on the topic "Priorities in Families." After I was done, the lone male in the room (whom I hadn't seen during my talk), an air force colonel, stood up and challenged me in front of everyone.

"Excuse me," he said, "but you obviously don't understand the air force. When a woman marries an air force officer, she understands that the air force must come first."

He went on a little bit longer, basically justifying why a man could totally ignore his family and put them on the bottom of the list as far as priorities go. I listened patiently until I couldn't take it anymore.

"I believe I *do* understand your air force," I said. "If you died tonight, your air force would have someone in your place by 0800 tomorrow morning."

Spontaneously every woman in that room got up and gave me a standing ovation; the colonel did an about-face and left.

Everyone is replaceable outside the home; no one is replaceable inside it. Don't sell your soul to the company store. If you do, there's still a great chance that your company will downsize, and you'll be out in the cold. Rather than sacrifice your kids on behalf of your career, be willing to make sacrifices in your career on behalf of your kids.

Remember:

- Constant criticism is a disruptive and ineffective style of parenting.
- Adolescents need some freedom; overcontrolling is a poor way to influence your kids.
- Sports are for fun and recreation; don't try to relive your life through your kids' exploits on the athletic fields.
- Career-driven parents miss what matters most—a rich and rewarding home life.

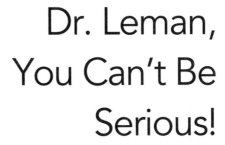

10

Dr. Leman, You Can't Be Serious!

SOMETIMES—OKAY, A *LOT* of times—I say things that could be considered provocative. I don't feel that I have done my job unless I've offended at least a few listeners and readers!

In this chapter I would like to highlight some of these sayings, particularly as they relate to adolescents. At first glance some of these beliefs may sound ridiculous, but hang with me for a while; you'll start to see the wisdom behind them.

Unhappy Kids Are Healthy Kids

In the very first chapter I spoke about the ridiculous optimism that many of today's kids have regarding their future financial portfolios. The sad truth behind that false optimism is, why shouldn't they feel that way? Many of today's adolescents have never been made to wait for anything. Whenever they had their heart set on something, it always came, many times without any sacrifice being made.

Why should wealth be any different?

Well, the answer is, the world isn't nearly as kind as parents are! When adolescents grow up with a strong sense of entitlement, they're headed for a rude awakening.

That's why I believe that occasionally unhappy kids are healthy kids. The world is an unhappy place, and the sooner our kids realize this, the better.

Frankly, as crazy as this sounds, I want my kids to be unhappy sometimes. Some things don't make us happy. As an adult, I have to go places and do things that I don't want to do, so why shouldn't I prepare my kids to do the same thing? It took Sande and me quite a long time to save up for our first house. When will my kids learn to save and put up with unfulfilled desires, if not in their family?

Although our youngest child, Lauren, isn't quite an adolescent, at nine years old she's certainly knocking on the door. Like so many kids, she wanted a razor scooter. "That's fine, Lauren," I said. "I've seen those, and I think you'd really enjoy one. Why don't you start saving your money?"

To be honest, Sande and I wouldn't even feel the $98 that it costs to buy a scooter. But even more important than having that scooter was Lauren's opportunity to learn a lesson.

Our nine-year-old diligently started saving her money—not a particularly easy thing to do when your allowance is only $2 a week. I was proud of her as she watched her stash slowly climb in value.

Finally after months of saving, Lauren still had just $49. Sande and I could easily have forked over the other $50 necessary to get Lauren that scooter, but we didn't. However, when my brother-in-law came to town, he heard her talking about this scooter she was saving up for and asked me if it was okay for him to buy her one as a birthday present.

I said yes, *on this basis:* Lauren had been working so hard to save her money that she had demonstrated responsibility, and my brother-in-law was going to give her a gift anyway.

Sande and I were willing to let Lauren wait, and that's the key.

It was okay with us if Lauren was unhappy about something because life has its trying moments.

This principle goes beyond delayed gratification, of course. Some of the most vivid memories of our daughter Holly's childhood are of the many times Sande took her along when she brought food baskets to a woman who lived in the barrio. This woman had a dirt floor and was extremely poor. These visits were not romanticized forays into social service, by any means. Holly smelled what a community is like when there isn't a sufficient sewage system. She learned that maybe it's not such a bad deal to have to sweep the floor, given that some families don't really have a floor to sweep. And she saw the sickness, the lack of adequate housing and clothing, and the deprivation that exists in some corners of this world.

The visits always made Holly a little unhappy, a little sad. When she walked into her own plush house and a bedroom that had more furniture than the entire adobe hut had, suddenly she felt a tinge of sobriety. I noticed that she was always a little more reserved those evenings.

Have your kids ever seen poverty? Have they ever been to a retirement center? If you shield them from these realities of life, they'll be ill-prepared for a responsible adulthood.

What You *Don't* Give Your Kids Is Very Important

"I own a Prada messenger bag, two Kate Spades, a Gucci belt and a Prada belt, and several pairs of Sisley jeans. I have a lot of Clinique makeup, Bobbi Brown eyeliner, MAC lip gloss, and Angel perfume—that's by Thierry Mugler."

Christina Shepp may be just eighteen years old, but, boy, does she know what's "in." On her wish list is a Prada nylon slicker, but since it comes with a price tag of $2,000, she reluctantly admits that getting it might be a bit of a stretch.[1]

Is this what we want our kids to value—the latest fashions and the highest-priced designer accessories?

Do you remember your relatively simple homecomings and proms? In my day a guy could really splurge on these big dates and still bring home change from a twenty. Those days are long gone! According to Patrick Welsh, a high school teacher, the homecoming weekend now involves dinner at an expensive restaurant and lavish hotel rooms for all-night parties. "But the big-time spending," Welsh continues, "comes with the senior prom, which can now cost more than some weddings."

Welsh drew duty to chaperone his school's prom in 1999. His description? "The orgy of extravagance . . . was . . . laughable. The entrance to the swank hotel where the dance was held was jammed with limousines, a fixture of the prom since the mid-80s. It has gotten to the point now where kids compete to see who will have the best limo.

"The winner this year was the new sixteen-passenger Lincoln Navigator. . . . One student told me that it cost only $175 for each of the eight couples who were chauffeured around."[2]

Notice *each* of the eight couples shelled out $175 to nab this elongated stretch of wheels, meaning this group of adolescents footed a $1,400 bill to rent a car *for one night*. When's the last time you've seen an adult do that?

I showed up at my date's house on prom night in 1960 driving a 1950 Ford that cost $200—just a little bit more than what each of these couples paid for a limo for one night. The heater in my Ford was broken, but secretly I thought this mechanical problem was a bonus—my date would have to get close and cuddly to stay warm! The girl's father saw the vehicle I drove up in and said to me, "You don't want to drive that old car. Why don't you take mine?" (I had a reputation as a nondrinker so I was actually pretty popular with the parents, which is how I was able to drive up to the prom in a brand-new 1960 Chevy.)

It was a simpler time back in the sixties. We wore suits and ties but didn't have to rent tuxes. The biggest expense for the evening was buying a corsage for our date. In fact, the entire night set most guys back no more than about twelve dollars. That's not true today, of course. One of the groups that Welsh was familiar with dined at the elegant and decidedly upscale Watergate Hotel, one of the most expensive restaurants in the Washington, D.C., area.

One thing about the prom night at Welsh's school was free however: condoms. These prophylactics were part of the "pre-prom package" available at the adolescent health clinic a few blocks from the school.

Welsh concludes—and I couldn't agree more—"I can't help but feel that we adults who acquiesce to the bigger and better party mentality of adolescents not only are contributing to the myth that you can't have fun without blowing a lot of money, but we also are creating a false sense of affluence that kids can't possibly sustain until they have jobs—and high-paying jobs at that—years from now."[3]

This sense of entitlement and affluence is putting adolescents on the course of financial disaster. The Consumer Federation of America released a study conducted by Georgetown University sociologist Robert Manning, who examined the "crisis" of credit-card debt among college students.[4] Credit-card companies have become almost ridiculously aggressive and are surprisingly open to risk. I remember attending a Buffalo Bills home game. Somebody was giving away Buffalo Bills padded seats, so I walked over to find out how to get one. The catch was that you had to fill out a credit-card application. I did so and forgot about it. Six weeks later, I got a Buffalo Bills credit card in the mail *with a $25,000 credit limit!*

There's something wrong in our society when you can fill out a thirty-second application and somebody hands you a $25,000 credit limit.

Apparently there aren't enough of us "adults" to take on this credit, so banks have begun marketing to college kids. Credit-card companies literally shower college kids with credit-card offers, and many students happily apply, procure the cards, tuck them into their wallets, and then use them.

And use them.

And use them some more.

The result? University of Indiana administrator John Simpson says that his university "lose[s] more students to credit-card debt than to academic failure." That's why Manning says that "marketing of credit cards on college campuses . . . poses a greater threat than alcohol or sexually transmitted diseases."[5]

I *almost* agree with Manning. I think the real problem isn't the marketing of credit cards but the lack of preparation that college students receive as adolescents, with the result that they don't know how to handle money.

I've often said that what you *don't* give your children is very important. Most parenting books are filled with chapters about what you *should* give to your children, but I think purposefully withholding certain items is just as essential. For instance, when I return from business trips, I don't come home with lots of presents. I want my kids to rejoice that their dad is home; why would I want to give them a toy that they'll want to go off and play with instead of spending their time with me?

I learned this early on. With my older kids, I often dropped off my bags by the door, grabbed a tackle box, and immediately took the family fishing. We talked more than we caught fish, but it was a great way to renew our relationship—and it was virtually free. If you asked my kids what they treasured most—some five- or ten-dollar plastic gizmo that would break in two hours or concentrated time with their dad out at the lake—I guarantee you they would choose the latter.

Tell me: If you spend $500 on your daughter's prom dress, what's she going to do when she gets her first job and has to buy three business dresses for about $100 total? What better time to teach her to get used to T.J. Maxx than now while she's still living at home?

If your son expects you to foot the $175 bill for a limo, when will he learn that life after school involves budgeting his money so that he can own a car *and* have enough money left over to rent an apartment?

Good parents don't just give good things to their kids. They also strategically withhold certain things from their kids. What you don't give to your adolescents is extremely important. Your kids don't need the material things you didn't have as a kid.

> What you don't give to your adolescents is extremely important. Your kids don't need the material things you didn't have as a kid.

Let's talk a bit more about what you can do to help your adolescents be financially responsible.

Money, Money, Money!

"Daddy," then seven-year-old Lauren asked me, "how's the Disney stock doing?"

I had to chuckle. How many fathers talk with their seven-year-old daughters about stocks? In fact, both of our youngest daughters own a few stocks. I've become more concerned about passing on wise financial management to my youngest children, in part because of a biological reality. I'm fifty-seven years old, and Lauren is nine, so I can't count on being around to "bail them out" (not that I would) if they don't learn these lessons on their own.

I'm frequently asked, "Should my teen get a job?" I have the same answer for every situation: "It depends."

Teens' first responsibility is to their home. Their second responsibility is to their school. If these two responsibilities are taken care of in an acceptable way, I have no problem with teens' earning a little extra cash, provided the job doesn't cut unduly into responsibilities numbers one and two.

I think certain jobs are inappropriate for teens in that they may alter a growing young man or young woman's schedule in a way that isn't healthy. For instance, I wouldn't let my sixteen-year-old son work as a busboy at a restaurant that kept him there until two o'clock in the morning.

Other factors to consider include your children's temperament and goals. If my son or daughter were studying an extra twenty hours a week in order to get into an Ivy League school, in addition to doing the requisite volunteer work and extracurricular activities that such admissions offices look for, I probably wouldn't want that child to work, at least not during the school year.

All of Sande's and my kids have worked during the summer, particularly at youth camps. Our thirteen-year-old daughter, Hannah, regularly baby-sits, but we carefully monitor those hours, particularly on school nights. Our oldest daughter, Holly, worked in a yogurt store, at her request. She came to me because she wanted more spending money, and since Holly cruised through school with top grades, we had no problem with her taking on a part-time job.

Krissy, on the other hand, didn't work during the school year because she was so heavily involved in sports. She literally went from one season to the next, and we felt that a job would impinge too much on the family time we had left over from her athletics.

So you see, we made our choices based on what was best for each individual child's situation.

Of course, earning money is just one aspect of money management; the other aspect is spending it. Money managers disagree on just about everything except this: Americans are doing a terrible job saving money.

When our kids were younger, I started matching whatever they decided to save. As always, I want to use "reality discipline," and employers often match contributions for employees; this is one way I could reinforce the long-term benefits of putting off impulse buying.

As far as allowances go, I believe kids get an allowance because they are members of the family, not for doing chores. They do chores because everybody needs to give back to the family. Now, if they fail to do their chores, I may well pay another child to do them and deduct the amount I pay out of their allowance, but in our family, allowances aren't directly tied to doing any work.

If you really want to teach your kids to manage their money well, though, you must be prepared to let them suffer. If your kid runs out of his allowance on Wednesday and desperately wants to go to the opening of the next Adam Sandler movie on Thursday, hold the line: "Payday is Saturday, Bub. You know that as well as I do. In two days, I'll be happy to give you the money, but not before then."

> Refuse to do anything that your kids should do for themselves.

If you give in and offer "credit," you're setting up your children to want the same thing when they become adults. You end up supporting the philosophy of the banks, which make obscene amounts of money from "adults" who pay ridiculously high rates of interest because they never learned how to budget their money and put a little away for emergencies.

Don't Do Things for Your Kids

Refuse to do anything that your kids should do for themselves. I'm not suggesting that as a parent you shouldn't do their laundry or fix their meals. But I am suggesting that kids' homework should actually be done by the kids! If you keep "covering" for your children, finishing up their reports, "touching up" their math assignments, here's what will happen: those same children will continue to place image over substance as they get older. They'll be all promise and no performance at work—and then be surprised when they get fired!

Responsible kids have learned that actions have consequences.

As a psychologist, I've learned that few things work as well as "shock value" to get this point across. For instance, if your daughter says something very hurtful—let's say she says, "I hate you," or she swears at you—don't fall apart. Maintain your composure, correct her, and then, when she comes to you later that day and reminds you that she needs the car to go to the dance, calmly say, "I'm sorry, Megan, but you're not going to the dance."

Megan is mystified. "What do you mean I'm not going to the dance? We talked about it last night, and you said I could go! I've already made plans. I'm supposed to pick up Sharon in fifteen minutes!"

"That's right, we did talk about it last night," you answer. "But that was before you spoke disrespectfully to me, which I don't appreciate, and I've decided that you're going to miss the dance."

Waiting until just the right moment will create a shock value that will really open this girl's ears. Dressed in her favorite dress, her hair all done up, makeup on, and completely ready to go out the door, she'll *never* forget this lesson—and she'll think twice before she mouths off to you (or a boss, a police officer, or some other authority) ever again.

I remain surprised at how controversial this advice seems to many of today's parents. Invariably when I mention a similar illustration in a seminar—such as making a teen miss a basketball game—someone will ask me, "What if my child is the star player? Is that fair to the team?"

Quite honestly I have to contain myself from laughing at these suggestions. Tell me, who won the Tucson Boys Club Basketball championship five years ago? Not one person in a million could tell you that *because in the long run it doesn't matter.*

How can a single basketball game ever be as important as a mother helping her son learn to respect women, beginning with his mom? If the other boys get angry, so much the better. The son will learn that his actions have wide-ranging consequences. I've talked to too many wives with husbands in jail—men who never considered how their "private" actions could affect their families.

If a mother isn't willing to make the call and then *stand her ground,* her son won't learn to respect her. Giving a boy some type of innocuous time-out certainly won't do it. Never forget: love and discipline are inseparable. It all comes down to balance. If you truly care about your children, you will learn to not do things for them. By the way, when a woman stands her ground with her son, she's not only teaching him to respect women but also doing a great service for her future daughter-in-law.

Remember:

- It is healthy for kids to be unhappy occasionally.
- What you don't give your kids is very important.
- Don't do everything for your kids.

11

The Dating Dance

DO YOU REMEMBER WHEN you fell in love? There's not a feeling like it in all the world. Now let's see, some of the things I remember about the first six times I fell in love are the excitement of getting a girlfriend, the thrill of giving her a friendship ring, and the disappointment at learning that she left it in the pocket of her jeans and it got totaled in the wringer washing machine.

Each time I fell in love, it seemed a little more wonderful than the time before. Of course, the "love" I'm talking about is what we commonly refer to as puppy love, but you couldn't have convinced me of that. No sir. This was the *real* thing, 100 percent, bona fide L-O-V-E. I knew this because "real love" always made my palms sweat.

You probably have your own stories of puppy love. Use those as an opportunity to tell your children some of the happy moments you had during your puppy-love experiences in your adolescent years. I think it really helps if we can tell kids, before they become adolescents, that they are probably going to experience some of the same things we did. They will meet someone who is so special that they won't be able to wait until morning to see him or her again—even if that means going to school. Puppy love makes young men suddenly become compulsive about brushing their teeth and combing their hair, and perhaps even sneaking a bit of their dad's aftershave. It makes a young girl stand in front of a mirror combing her hair into perfection or plotting how to stay home "sick" from school simply because she has a pimple that she'd "just die" if Jimmy saw.

Tell some of the funny stories about the crazy things you did to get someone's attention. Share how you learned to get over heartbreak. Let your kids see that they aren't the first, and they won't be the last, who have to kayak their way through the white water of young love. Just wait until you hear how I finally met my wife!

When I Found Love

I met my wife in the men's room at the Tucson Medical Center in Arizona. I was a janitor, and she was a nurse's aide. I knew there was something special about Sande from the very beginning, but actually starting a conversation with her proved to be a little difficult. On a few occasions we passed each other in the hallway and she said hello, but I could never quite muster up any response other than "good morning."

Then came the day I'll never forget. I was cleaning the men's room, so I put out one of those mobile trash barrels in the lavatory doorway to let everyone know the rest room was being cleaned. Just as I was emptying some trash into the barrel at the door, Sande came around the corner.

Our eyes met and locked. This was my chance. With all the tact of a bull, I blurted out, "Do you want to go to the world's fair with me?"

Sande was understandably confused. We were in Tucson, and the world's fair that year was being held in New York.

"Pardon me?" Sande asked.

Since New York was a little far, we settled on going out to lunch. It was on me. I ordered one McDonald's cheeseburger and cut it in half with a plastic fork (my kids love this part). My stomach was doing so many flip-flops that I couldn't even finish my half. Sande was so special, I shook inside just looking at her.

It's hard to believe, but that was almost forty years ago, and though I've been known to eat much more than half a cheese-burger in Sande's presence since then, I can still recall the intoxication of those first few months of dating.

What a time it was!

Of course, those feelings never last. Our initial infatuation with each other grew into a steady, loving relationship with which we're both very happy.

How can we help our young adolescents learn to keep their own intense infatuations in perspective? I like to use something that writers through the ages have called the "love chapter."

Love Song

One of the most famous chapters in the Bible is 1 Corinthians 13, where the apostle Paul describes the criteria for true love. After reading enough psychological material to put an entire generation to sleep for a decade, I've yet to come across anything that addresses the topic so thoroughly and so practically. Paul tells us what love is and what it is not. He then follows that up with what love does not do and then ends with what love does. In case you haven't read this passage in a while, here is an excerpt:

> Love is patient and kind. Love is not jealous or boastful or proud or rude. Love does not demand its own way. Love is not irritable, and it keeps no record of when it has been wronged. It is never glad about injustice but rejoices whenever the truth wins out. Love never gives up, never loses faith, is always hope-ful, and endures through every circumstance. (vv. 4-7, NLT)

Let's look at this masterful piece of writing—applicable to people of all faiths.

Love is patient. One thing that dating does for young people, if they approach dating with the right attitude, is give their relationship a test of time. All of us tend to want instant gratification, so naturally adolescents often seek instant intimacy. Unfortunately there's no such thing. Love is *patient.* Love needs time to get to know the other person. True love can wait until marriage for physical intimacy.

The key here, I think, is not to deny the wonderful feelings associated with an infatuation but rather to get your teens to think about how to nurture love out of that intense sensation. Warn your adolescents: "You're going to *feel* as if you want to give this person everything, but remember, true love is *patient.* If you truly love each other, you'll wait for each other. There'll be no pressuring."

The best comeback for the old standby "If you love me, you'll sleep with me" is, "If you love *me,* you'll wait until we get married!"

Love is kind. A person who has read many of my books and heard me speak on numerous occasions brought to my attention a radio "shock jock" who is taking the country by storm. This Howard Stern wanna-be calls himself a "professor" and seeks to give guidance about how men and women should conduct themselves in relationships. One of the things he's famous for is encouraging men to act like jerks. "That's the kind of man most women want," this guy says. "Don't buy her flowers. Don't call her on the phone. Tell her all you want is sex, and if that's not okay with her, you'll find someone else."

Sadly there *are* women like this out there; the worse you treat them, the more they'll fall for you. But these aren't the type of women you want your sons to marry. Their esteem is crushed. They have often suffered sexual abuse. And although they may act like sexual gymnasts before marriage, as soon as they tie the knot, their sexual ardor almost always dies on the spot.

True love is kind. True love buys flowers. True love calls

when you're going to be late or when you have to break a date. True love is considerate and thoughtful. True love is willing to do the unpleasant.

The reason it's so important to stress this to our adolescents is that they can be treated in the worst way but still believe their persecutor if he says he "loves" them. We need to show our children that love is kind. If a person treats them rudely, routinely stands them up, makes fun of them, and is interested only in sex, it's not love, regardless of the words he uses.

> Love never demands its own way.

Love is not jealous or boastful or proud or rude. Do your teenagers feel threatened when someone is around the people they are dating? When a person of the opposite sex talks to your teenagers' special friend, do they get a little sick feeling in the stomach? That's jealousy. True love trusts the other and is not jealous.

In the same way, true love isn't selfish. Does your daughter's boyfriend insist on always doing what he likes to do? Do they always have to hang around his friends? That's selfish. That's not love.

Go over each of these qualities with your adolescents—help them learn to discern the true nature of the person who has captured their heart.

Love does not demand its own way. Love never "gets back" at the other or tries to "get even." Love never demands its own way. I think if I could pick one part of the love chapter to measure all relationships with, it would be this one: Love does not demand its own way. The other person's feelings and needs are more important.

This is the exact opposite of how most kids who are infatuated feel. They are on top of the world. They've never been so happy. They're literally in love with being in love, and they can't get enough of it. As a parent, you'll have to put up with those smiles that come out of nowhere, those sighs that occur throughout the day, and your daughter's belief that she will "die, absolutely die a horrible, cruel, pained death" if she can't see her boyfriend for a twenty-four-hour stretch.

Love is not irritable. It's the little things about our loved ones that drive us up a wall. Teenagers and their dates often argue over stupid things. Really big arguments can be touched off over minuscule misunderstandings. Real love overcomes all this.

Allow me to let you in on what's really happening during so many of these adolescent "breakups." Both the boy and girl fall in love with a fantasy. That fantasy is lovely, too good to be true, and it is! It's like a soap bubble, fascinating to watch but headed for a very short life. As soon as reality intrudes on the kids' fantasy and that bubble pops, they blame each other. "You're not who you said you were!" is a common accusation.

Love keeps no record of when it has been wronged. The kind of love Paul is talking about here is a love that can forgive. When reality sets in, the person who truly loves holds no grudges. Love doesn't search the past to come up with more "ammunition" for the next verbal war. It forgives and moves on.

Love is never glad about injustice but rejoices whenever the truth wins out. Love never gives up, never loses faith, is always hopeful, and endures through every circumstance. A relationship that is not built on truth will never be a lasting relationship. A life built on anything other than total honesty is eventually going to run into a wall. If we really love someone, we will be loyal to that person no matter what the cost. We will always believe in that person, always expect the best, and always stand our ground in defending him or her.

What does all this mean? Just as our kids need help in learning how to read words and figure out mathematical equations, so they need help in learning how to discern true love. The best training will be done before infatuation sets in. If you wait until your Romeo has found his Juliet before you start talking about the difference between love and lust, infatuation and genuine commitment, you're going to have an enormously difficult time trying to get yourself heard. But if you start talking to your son and daughter well before they enter adolescence, then you can rejoice with them when they find someone special and have a calm conversation about the person's qualities and what might make the person a good friend to have.

If you sense that your daughter is in a destructive relationship, it's best to approach the matter sensitively and indirectly. I'd say something like this:

"You know, honey, I could be wrong [by the way, I love to use that phrase—it softens your advice and opens up your kid's ears], but it seems that there have been four or five times this past week that David said he was going to come over but then didn't. I don't know him as well as you do, but I'm wondering if he has a problem with following through. His word doesn't seem as good as it could be, and I was wondering if that bothers you?"

What these few sentences accomplish is to tell your teen that you know what's going on, you're concerned, and that you have a good understanding of the pain and hurt she feels inside. In a backdoor fashion you're empathizing with your daughter but not trying to run her life.

Be patient, however. It might take another three months for your daughter to see David for what he is. All you can do is plant the seeds of doubt in her mind. Ultimately she is going to have to make the decision.

As your family eats the evening meal or takes a weekend drive, crack open this book and spend some time discussing the qualities outlined in the previous paragraphs. If you can familiarize your preadolescents with the nature of what love truly is, they'll be better prepared to keep the inevitable infatuations in perspective.

The Dating Dance

Dating has suddenly become controversial. One of the best-selling books for teens over the past several years is entitled

I Kissed Dating Goodbye, followed by a book that issued a counter-challenge, *I Gave Dating a Chance.*

I've met Joshua Harris, the author of *I Kissed Dating Goodbye,* and I think he makes some very good points. On the other hand, I also believe dating in today's society is a very appropriate way to get to know which qualities you are looking for in a lifetime marriage partner.

In fact, I like to shock seminar participants by boldly and confidently proclaiming, "I believe teenagers should be intimate in their dating."

Only after the jaws drop open do I add, "but not physically intimate."

What I mean by *intimate* is that as a young man begins to date one young woman more than any other, both of them should have the goal to discover as many things about each other as they can. What does the other value most in life? Is this a person who puts people ahead of things? Is this someone who will make family a priority? What are this person's spiritual values? Is this a nurturing person—a giver or a taker? Can this person take off the mask and let the other see the real person without getting that feeling of rejection?

Not a single one of these questions can be answered in bed. All of them are best discussed while fully clothed! That's what I mean by being *truly* intimate.

Dating also provides an opportunity to help our kids think about others. Connie broke Greg's heart when she told him, "I'm breaking up with you, not because you've done anything wrong, but because I've never really felt anything for you. My mom likes you—you're the class president, after all—but now I see that's not enough, at least not for me."

Rarely are teens so honest! One of the saddest and most troubling aspects of early dating is that it is so self-centered. An adolescent lusts for status as much as anything else, and status has everything to do with "being with the right person." Often, there is very little emotional feeling for the dating partner, just a desire to be seen with the right someone—a cheerleader, the quarterback, any popular person. If an adolescent male can snag a date with a very attractive young woman, he becomes known as an attractive young man, and vice versa.

Everybody, at any age, wants to be noticed. Nobody wants to be a neutral, invisible nonperson. And adolescents, in particular, crave attention.

This might sound odd, but this lust for attention creates a great opportunity for you to turn the tables and teach your teen to notice *others.* Author and former basketball star Jay Carty tells a true story about a young woman who created a highlight for a young boy who had terrible difficulties. Susan was everybody's choice to take to the dance; Jimmy was, at best, tolerated. You see, Jimmy had faced a terrible bout with cancer that left him with a reconstructed chin and no lips. When he ate, he had to put a napkin to his mouth, or some of the food would fall out. Obviously Jimmy wasn't the first choice for most of the girls contemplating a dinner-dance date.

But Susan made a memory that Jimmy will never forget when she asked him to accompany her to the dance. She didn't lead Jimmy on, pretending that they were going to be boyfriend and girlfriend, but she put her hand through Jimmy's arm as the two walked into the hall, much to everyone's amazement. For a night Jimmy felt like a prom king.

I like to tell kids that there are two kinds of people: those who work hard to be noticed and those who work hard to notice others. Those who work hard to be noticed always end the night feeling frustrated because they are never noticed *enough.* Those who concentrate on noticing others are usually the most fulfilled because there are always people who need to be noticed, and when you act unselfishly, you gain self-respect, self-esteem, and quiet pleasure.

When your kids return from a date, watch what you say.

Instead of just going over the events of the evening, ask them if they had had a chance to talk with anyone who seemed to need a word of encouragement or just a friend to talk to. Let them benefit from your concern for the often ignored, and perhaps it will rub off on them.

I obviously believe that dating has its place, but I also think it's important to delay the dating dance as long as possible.

Delaying the Dance

This might surprise some of you, but from what I have discovered in working with families, many kids start dating because their parents push them into it, sometimes at a very early age. While many adults deny this, simply ask yourself: Have you ever heard an adult say to a seven-year-old child (maybe even yours), "Do you have a girlfriend [boyfriend] yet?"

What does this convey to a youngster? "Gee, it sounds like it's time to get a steady. That must be what growing up is all about."

Added to this is the even weightier pressure brought by peers. For some reason today's kids aren't allowed the luxury of being just friends with the opposite sex. As soon as a boy and girl start talking—even in the lower grades—their playmates will start teasing them: "Two little lovebirds sitting in a tree . . ."

By the time children reach junior high, social events quickly put the dating mind-set into play. And by high school—where the premier social events of the year revolve around dating opportunities—dating takes on extreme importance.

I'm not naïve; it may be impossible to delay dating much past junior high. But I do think parents should make every effort to encourage healthy friendships for as long as possible, even past the dating years. If your children mention a friend of the opposite sex, encourage their socializing without using the label "boyfriend" or "girlfriend." Let your children get to know the opposite sex without all the baggage that comes with dating.

I can hear some of you shouting at the book, "Enough about

the generalities, Leman! I want the specifics! What's appropriate and when?"

God didn't make me the dating guru, but if you want my advice, I'm happy to oblige. Of course, each individual kid is different, but in general, I think dating can begin *in groups* around fourteen or fifteen years old. Any younger than that is too young. I had a fifteen-year-old girl tell me once that she was "absolutely bored" with dating. She started so young that she kept progressing further and further in order to keep the dating experience "exciting." Now she was so sick of getting drunk, stoned, smashed, and making out that she'd had it. She wanted time out from guys—and she needed it!

A boy or girl fourteen or fifteen years old doesn't need "alone time" with the opposite sex. It's too early to get physical. Physical touch is, by its nature, progressive, and since a fifteen-year-old is probably ten years away from marriage (at least), there's no use heating things up too soon. I'd hold the line at group dating here, and I'd make sure that there would be some type of supervision at all times. For instance, couples don't need to go to remote places—pairing off and making out in front of others occurs without shame these days—so if a group really wants to talk, they should go to a Denny's or a pizza place.

> Dating should be a time of having fun, sharing time with somebody else, and getting to know each other.

Sixteen is a good age for adolescents to begin dating one-on-one, but here again, I wouldn't just turn my daughter loose! Dating should be a time of having fun, sharing time with somebody else, and getting to know each other. But your teenager is going to need some help in setting guidelines. Those of you who have read my previous books won't be surprised to hear me say that you should encourage your adolescents to prepare their own guidelines for dating before they go out on their first date. The discussion will go something like this:

Daughter: "Dad, I've been sixteen for almost three weeks now—well, two weeks and five days—and I think it's time I should be allowed to date a boy one-on-one."

Dad: "I agree. Do you have someone in mind, or do you need me to pick him out for you?"

Daughter: "I think I can handle it, Dad. In fact, Jon Clark asked me to go to the movies this Friday."

Dad: "Jon Clark? Didn't I see his name and picture on the back of a milk carton this morning?"

Daughter: "Daaad."

Dad: "Okay, honey. But before you go out with Jon "Milk Carton" Clark, I want you to draw up your own guidelines for dating, and we'll discuss them Thursday night."

Daughter: "What kind of guidelines?"

Dad: "Well, these would be the guidelines you think are appropriate for a young woman your age. I want you to think about where you'll go and won't go, what you'll do and won't do, how you'll choose your dates, and what you'll do in touchy situations."

Daughter: "What do you mean by 'touchy' situations?"

Dad: "You know exactly what I mean. What if your boyfriend starts drinking? What if he tries to take off your shirt? That kind of thing."

Daughter: "Okay."

Dad: "Remember: if I don't have your guidelines by Thursday, there'll be no date on Friday."

Most kids basically know the problems that exist with dating, and most of them really don't want to get themselves into a situation they can't handle. What happens is that they get "caught" in spur-of-the-moment situations. For instance, what if the girl is at a party with her date and he starts drinking and then wants to take her home? She should consider *ahead of time* how she's going to respond. What if the boy begins pressuring her to have sex? She needs to think about this before it actually happens, even if she's dating a "nice" boy.

Since your children have created these guidelines, your job as the parent is simply to help them live up to them. This makes your job all the easier, as teens won't rebel quite so quickly against their own guidelines.

For instance, I know of a sixteen-year-old girl whose parents allowed her to set her own curfew at midnight. Let me tell you, those parents were pleasantly surprised to find their daughter coming home from her dates at ten or eleven. This is not at all unusual when teenagers are trusted to set some of their own guidelines. So let them prepare a list of dos and don'ts. I think that's a far healthier way to start than for Mom and Dad to issue an edict on how things are going to be.

One thing I know from working with young people on a professional basis for three decades is that if they have any input into rules and regulations, there's a higher probability that they will adhere to them. Of course, there will have to be some discussion between parents and kids as you refine the list, and probably some give-and-take as well. But let your kids take the first step.

Marriage Myths That Lead to Misery

One other thing that you can help your adolescents understand is some of the things you've learned from watching other marriages. In an attempt to help your teens avoid problems, share with them the following—and other—marriage myths.

"He [or she] will change after we get married."

This is probably the most frequent marriage myth that I hear expressed in the counseling room. I can safely say that there is almost no chance of changing someone after you're married. In fact, what bothers you most is likely to *intensify* after you tie the knot.

Look at it this way: your daughter's boyfriend probably knows that his drinking, smoking, gambling, cussing—or whatever—bugs your daughter. He's been trying to limit it as best he can because he truly wants to marry Susie. Once he already has Susie, why should he change? Now he can relax and really be himself!

I've seen this happen time after time. Parents, you must help your children look honestly at their boyfriends or girlfriends, and be frank with them: What you see is what you get. You can't expect it to ever be as good as this, because people generally put their best foot forward while they are dating.

"This is what love feels like."

Our children need to know that there's a tremendous difference between "falling in love" and "falling in need."

Kathy and Ron were extremely young when they got married, both sixteen. Kathy was escaping an unhealthy situation in her home. Her father was abusive, and she was desperate for male attention, affection, and "love."

Ron was equally unhappy. His mom was an alcoholic, as selfish as they come, and verbally abusive. Ron melted in Kathy's feminine arms of approval and desire.

The two lovebirds were literally forced together by their needs. Unfortunately at sixteen neither was mature enough to love unselfishly. Perhaps unconsciously, but just as factually, they were in the marriage to get their needs met. When two children were added to the mix and the physical ardor died down, the relationship fell apart. Kathy wasn't getting her needs met, and Ron wasn't getting his needs met. Their insecurities had brought them together, but insecurity can never *hold* a marriage together. The two ended up getting a divorce.

You never solve a problem by getting married. In fact, you

usually create new problems. Marriage is the place to learn to love someone unconditionally, until one of you dies. It is not a place to run to simply to have your needs met—be they affection, sex, money, or acceptance.

Adolescence can be an exciting time. Your children are going to begin making choices that will affect them for the rest of their lives. Perhaps no choice is quite as significant as the person whom they marry. Embrace this challenge. Do your best to prepare them to make a wise choice.

Remember:

- Kids need training so that they can understand the nature of true love.
- Teens need to be taught how to judge character, rather than to focus on feelings.
- Parents often unintentionally speed up the dating process.
- Adolescents should draw up their own dating guidelines.
- Bad habits tend to get worse, not better, after the wedding.
- There's a tremendous difference between "falling in love" and "falling in need."

12

Sex and the Adolescent

I WAS IN CHICAGO on a tour for my book *Sex Begins in the Kitchen,* so I called a bookstore to make sure it had plenty of copies. A female clerk answered the phone, and I asked, "Do you have *Sex Begins in the Kitchen?*"

There was a short pause, followed by a boisterous scream, "Where I have sex is none of your business!"

She heard "Do you have sex?" and "kitchen," and that was enough for her!

Whenever I am speaking to an audience and mention sex, the room gets almost eerily quiet; then, when I say something funny about sex, the audience laughs with gusto. The topic of sex seems to release pent-up emotions. Even as adults we're not all that comfortable talking about it—especially when talk about sex concerns what our kids may be doing behind closed doors.

But this is talk that needs to take place! I am a firm advocate in saving sexual relations until marriage. Unfortunately fewer and fewer "experts" agree with me on this. Teen sexual activity is so high that many counselors have given in and now advocate teaching "safe sex" over abstinence.

The problem with this approach is that no condom will protect a young woman's heart. I see the casualties of premarital sex in my office on a regular basis. Sexual activity before marriage has grave consequences—emotionally, physically, and spiritually. We'll cover all of these in detail later on, but I want to put my presupposition up front: Sexual activity before marriage is a great way for adolescents to get themselves in a lot of trouble.

What's Going On
In our grandparents' world, young men and women got married rather early—their late teens—just as they were coming into their sexual prime. Today's teens face a double-edged sword; not only do they experience puberty and sexual maturation at a younger age, but marriage is now often postponed until the mid- to late twenties, leaving many young people with a ten-year gap between the rise of sexual interest and their availability for marriage.

The result of this gap is that today's teens are, sadly, very sexually active. An example is a fifteen-year-old former client named Shelly, who made a bet with her friend Samantha over who could lose her virginity first. Unfortunately for Shelly, she won the "race."

In Shelly's own words, her first sexual experience "hurt like hell." Her date was very drunk, and when he was done, he treated her like a used Kleenex, actually leaving her in a dark park and driving himself home.

As surprising as this may seem to some parents, in many circles of young people today it really is a "cool" thing to lose your virginity, and the earlier the better. When young men gather in high schools across the country every Monday morning, many conversations begin like this: "So how far did you get with Sheila?" "Did anybody score on Friday or Saturday?"

This isn't particularly new. I went to high school with a boy who actually put "notches" in his belt—and you can guess what those notches represented!

Just how sexually active are today's teens? Perhaps the most reliable source is the U.S. Government's Centers for Disease Control. Through surveys conducted every other year, these researchers have compiled a general picture of exactly what types of sexual behavior our teenagers (grades 9–12) are getting involved in.

In 1997–the latest year for which data has been released– almost half of the males and females had experienced sexual intercourse. Seventeen percent of the males and 24 percent of the females admitted having four or more sex partners during their lifetime. About one-third of the males and slightly more than one-third of the females admitted that they were "currently sexually active," which means they had had sexual intercourse in the three months preceding the survey.

> **If your teenagers graduate from high school as virgins, they are now exceptions.**

Unfortunately these numbers keep rising as the students get older. By twelfth grade 60 percent have had sexual intercourse, and almost half (46 percent) are currently sexually active.[1] By the time adolescents turn twenty, more than eight in ten have had intercourse.[2]

This means that if your teenagers graduate from high school as virgins, they are now exceptions. If they make it into their junior year of college as virgins, they are among the rare 20 percent of their peers.

Just as alarming, teens are getting much more liberal about activities that they don't define as "sex." Thanks in no small part to a former high-ranking government official, most teens today don't consider oral sex as "having sex." Researchers have been shocked to find that teens who are pledged to "abstinence" still engage in this extremely intimate activity without calling it sex. Many sexually transmitted diseases, including oral herpes and gonorrhea of the pharynx, can still be caught during oral sex. As a psychologist I would add that experiencing sexual climax with another person, even without actual intercourse, has major emotional consequences.

A December 2000 report in *Family Planning Perspectives,* published by the Alan Guttmacher Institute, concludes that "there has been an overall increase in oral sex. And it is a reasonable assumption that it has increased in our youngest teens."[3] Robert Blum, director of the division of general pediatrics and adolescent health at the University of Minnesota-Twin Cities, states, "Most younger teens, even 10- to 12-year-olds, and maybe most teens (in general) don't define this as sex."[4]

One counselor explained to a reporter, "Clinton said oral sex isn't sex. Kids tell me over and over in my office, the president did it."[5] So they're doing it too—in droves.

This much sexual activity inevitably leads to peer pressure and ridicule. A boy isn't thought to be a "man" until he's had his first "woman." In fact, the word *virgin* is often used as a general way to put down another classmate, as in "He's such a virgin."

Another dirty little secret that doesn't get nearly the amount of press that it should is how many young women have voluntary *but unwanted* sex. That is, they ultimately give their consent, so it's not technically rape, but when asked, these girls say that they didn't really want to experience intercourse. The Alan Guttmacher Institute states that 70 percent of girls who had sex before age thirteen fall into this category.[6]

In the midst of this climate can you afford to be silent with your children and "hope" they make it through high school with their purity intact? Absolutely not. So what's the solution? Begin talking with your children about sex even before they reach adolescence.

How Do I Talk about Sex?

I know it's difficult to talk to anyone about sex, and it's even more difficult to talk with your children about the topic. It would be so much easier if we could just slip an informational brochure under our teenagers' doors and attach a note that says, "If you have any questions at all about sex, please feel free to contact me at my office, using my toll-free phone number."

But you see, teenagers need more than just information. What adolescents need as much as anything is love, understanding, and a commitment on their parents' part to get involved in their lives.

First off, it is essential to frame sex in a positive light. So often, because we want kids to avoid premarital sex, we frame all sex as bad when we should be affirming the high nature of its pleasure. I would try to talk to a son like this: "Sex is good, Barry. In fact, it's great! It feels really special to touch someone like that and to be touched like that. To be honest, Barry, although there are a lot of good feelings in life—like biting into a charcoal-broiled cheeseburger or tasting warm chocolate chip cookies right out of the oven—they all pale in comparison to the great feeling of sex. And someday you'll really enjoy this with your wife."

Some of you are saying, "Won't talking this way make them want to experience sex before marriage?" No, because the second way you frame sex is always within the concept of marriage. Denying the goodness of sex is futile. When a girl sits in Barry's lap, and he feels himself becoming aroused, *not that big a deal* isn't the thought that comes to his mind. What he's thinking is, *Wow! This is incredible! Unbelievable!*

If you paint sex as bad, you'll lose Barry's trust. You have to forewarn him that sex can be very exhilarating, one of the most powerful experiences he'll ever know. Otherwise, he'll be caught off guard and think, *If my parents lied about this, maybe they didn't know what they were talking about when they said I should wait until marriage. Maybe there's something wrong with them, and they've never experienced sexual feelings like this before.*

This is just one reason why I can't think of a better way to become involved with your teenagers than to share some of your real-life experiences that will show your teenagers that you are not really the product of the Dark Ages, that you have faced sexual temptation yourself, and that you realize the many struggles and temptations they face. What this kind of honest disclosure does is to help your teens know that you are *with* them rather than *against* them. You want them to ultimately have a wonderful and fulfilling sex life—in the appropriate place and time.

As an added bonus, when you're brave enough to share some experiences from your own life, then your teenagers *might* be willing to share some real thoughts and feelings with you too.

"That sounds fine, Dr. Leman," some of you might be saying, "but *how* do I begin talking about sex when I've never brought it up before?"

Ideally you'll start the process when your children are young. Not only will this make it easier for you to raise the topic later on, but it will help your children deal with their normal sexual curiosity in a healthy, noncondemning way.

Find a book that appropriately displays what a human body looks like, and show it to your children without embarrassment. Ignorance isn't bliss in this department. Answer all questions honestly and accurately. Moms, some of you might have to practice in front of a mirror before you can say the words *penis* or *vagina* out loud in front of your children, but learn to do so. From the very start—from the time your children are just five or six years old—you want them to know that sex is a wonderful gift *expressed between a husband and a wife.* The thought that sex would ever be explored outside marriage should sound odd and demeaning—because it is.

As your children approach the dating age, it's time to get more specific and to impart some strategies to help them remain sexually pure. Talk about how you and your spouse learned to control your own sex drives. Read through some Bible passages that talk about the importance of self-control as well as the joy of married sexuality. Be frank, honest, open, affirming, and noncondemning.

If you haven't been having these conversations before, I suggest that you begin by taking your daughter or son out for lunch or dinner. Let your teenager choose the restaurant, have a good time, and along the way, make a few attempts—feeble as they might be—to begin broaching the subject.

If the thought of a heavy conversation with your son or daughter is too scary even to think about, start with something light. My kids know all about the time I ripped off the conscience fund or how my mom always screamed at me when she found live bait in the pockets of my jeans. They know I wasn't a perfect kid, and in fact they thoroughly enjoy listening to the dumb, foolish things I did as a teenager.

Although my wife and I were both virgins on our wedding day, we can still talk about the temptations we faced and what we did to overcome them. I don't pretend that I had no sexual desire or that such a thing never crossed my mind.

Many pop psychologists like to insist that such meaningful conversations have to be eyeball-to-eyeball, but I couldn't disagree more! When you're talking to your daughter about sex, there's something very refreshing about driving down the interstate, looking at that blurry white line, while you force yourself to broach topics and enunciate words that embarrass you. And quite frankly your fourteen-year-old daughter, just a few years into her training bra, loves the fact that she can look out the passenger window of the car, rolling her eyes and thinking to herself, *I can't believe I'm having this conversation with my dad.* Never underestimate the value of driving in a car while having difficult conversations! I'm not just a psychologist—I'm a dad who is rearing five children, and I've had to learn some lessons the hard way.

Once the topic is out in the open, you can consider a more comprehensive time, such as a weekend away with just you and your child. Before you jump to the conclusion that dads should take the boys and moms should take the girls, let me dispel such a notion right now. I'm a big fan of the opposite-sex parent doing the bulk of the talking. As a counselor I've seen too many young women who were "taught" all about sex by their mothers, who knew even less than the daughter did! Who better understands how a woman thinks and feels, and how her body reacts and responds, than a boy's mother? And who can better explain to a young woman how easily a boy can get excited than her dad? In this safe, nonsexual environment, adolescents can ask questions firsthand.

Think just for a moment about where you got all your information about sex. If you're like most people, you got it from misinformed friends, dirty stories, pornographic magazines, and even rest-room walls. Personally the *National Geographic* magazine was the primer that my lifelong friend Moonhead and I used! Research tells us that, sadly, only a very few people are privileged enough to get good, honest, and accurate information in the safe confines of a loving home and from a caring parent. Wouldn't you like to bless your children with this healthy start in their sexual development?

I know it's difficult to find time for these things, no less so for me than for you. I've faced this challenge by taking one of my children with me on a business trip when I'm conducting a seminar or doing a television program in another city. I make sure that we have plenty of time for fun, but invariably, as we're eating, or resting in our hotel room, we also have numerous opportunities for serious talk. Any of my kids would happily forsake his or her own activities to hop on an airplane and go with me. We always come back closer and with a better understanding of each other, and we both feel as if it was well worth it.

If you're too busy to take time out for things like this, I've got news for you: you're *too* busy, and you need to cut some things out of your schedule. If you truly want your children to have a healthy attitude and lifestyle regarding sexuality, you need to become more involved in your children's lives. A government study found that adolescents are most likely to adopt their parents' attitudes about teen sex if the parents frequently discuss sex-related topics and seem comfortable doing so.[7] Psychologist Daniel Whitaker of the Centers for Disease Control warns that if parents never talk about sex, the kids aren't as likely to have an accurate perception of their parents' sexual attitudes and will be far less inclined to share them.[8]

During this study two things marked those adolescents who most closely shared their parents' values. They said their parents had talked frequently about numerous sex-related topics, including normal sexual development and maturation, but also about things like birth control and sexually transmitted diseases. They also said that their parents seemed "skilled and open" when discussing sex, making them feel comfortable during the talks. If you can create such an atmosphere in your own home, your teenagers will be among the lucky few, the true minority who grow up in a healthy environment in which they can learn to discover and control their sexual desires.

We've already discussed the "hows"—talking in the car, going away on trips, eating dinner at a restaurant—so let's discuss *what* needs to be addressed.

Help Your Children Choose Purity

One of my more popular talks for young people is entitled, "Help! I've Got a Rocket in My Pocket!" Kids love it because I do things they don't expect me to do—like asking them to give me the most popular names for the male genitalia. It takes them a while to get warmed up, but soon they really get rolling. You could hear a pin drop, however, when I suddenly shift gears and ask, "Great! Now what do we call the female genitalia?"

After the silence goes on and on, I ask, "Why is everybody so quiet? Could it be that those names sound dirty and vulgar? Could it be that they cheapen and demean the beauty of sexual love?"

I talk about the stuff that seems obvious to you and me but that many young adolescents have never considered. For instance,

I explain to young women how young men can get turned on in 3.4 seconds (that would be on a slow day, of course). If Susie comes downstairs to meet her date and is wearing a low-cut blouse, I can guarantee that Sammy will spend half the movie looking down instead of up.

When you think about it, boys want to engage in sexual activity for only one reason: it feels good. If sex were painful, young men would gladly wait until marriage to conceive children. Young women have other reasons—pursuing an artificial intimacy, not wanting the boy to leave them—but many of them are also in pursuit of pleasure. Since pleasure is the primary motive behind sexual activity, the more reasons you can give your children to abstain from sexual activity before they get married, the more prepared they'll be to resist the powerful allure of perhaps the most intense pleasure in all of human experience.

Let's look at some of the best reasons to abstain, points you'll want to raise in various conversations with your adolescents.

Religious Values
A recent article in the *Arizona Republic* contained this encouraging start:

> Faith Shepherd went to her prom with 29 of her friends. Each one of the Mormon teens had a date, but none went as a mushy, romantic, kissy-face couple. . . .
>
> Lubna Ahmad, a 13-year-old Muslim, is more interested in music and math than boys. She plans to stay focused on classes at Corona del Sol High School in Tempe, and when she's ready to marry, she will follow Muslim guidelines in choosing a husband. . . .
>
> Josh Harris, 23, kissed his fiancée for the first time on October 3—after they were pronounced husband and wife. Harris is a Christian and national speaker on sexual purity before marriage.[9]

What all of these adolescents have in common is a foundational faith experience that has grounded them in the things that matter most. Faith Shepherd said, "Now isn't the time to find my husband. It's a time to find the qualities I want in a husband." Religious values reinforce teens' decisions to say no to sexual activity.

If you truly want your kids to postpone sexual activity until marriage, it helps for them to have a belief that transcends *you*. You can't follow them into the backseat on their dates, but God can. Believing in a God who is ever present is a very powerful reality for an adolescent.

Pointing Out Painful Consequences

I'm not one who believes that sexual education can be accomplished in a single moment. Teaching abstinence is best done by alertly looking out for what I call "the teachable moments of life." For example, let's say you hear one of your children whispering about the fifteen-year-old schoolmate who got pregnant. She was a top volleyball player as a sophomore, and she always dreamed of playing volleyball for a southern California school. Instead of giving your child a sermon here, I would simply ask, "How do you think she'll ever get a chance to play college volleyball now?"

If you communicate with your children, you'll find any number of situations in which the reality of life comes right in your face. Yes, it's uncomfortable for us to talk about fifteen-year-old girls who get pregnant, but as parents it's our duty to use these occasions to reinforce what we've already taught.

After asking the above question, I might add, "Boy, I guess getting caught up in passion and letting emotions rule

> If you truly want your kids to postpone sexual activity until marriage, it helps for them to have a belief that transcends *you.*

your life, even for one night, really can have some pretty painful consequences."

As much as you may want to stick your head in the sand, you've got to bring the slimy world out into the open and even discuss it at the dinner table. Most of us parents don't want to do that; we want to keep our kids under the glass and pretend that they are safe and protected. But they're not. We have to help them see how much potential they have to mess up their lives.

I stress to my kids that they are in what I call the "Titanic Trigger Years" of their life. What I mean by this is that a single split-second decision—like having sex in the backseat even though neither partner planned on it—can change their lives forever. One drunken spree, one time on drugs—these "little" decisions can have titanic consequences and threaten their most cherished dreams.

Teaching Why Abstinence Is Best

Adolescents should choose abstinence for lots of reasons. It's "talking in volumes" to try to explain all of these in one sitting, but over the course of a year or so, take advantage of "teachable" moments to remind your teens of each reason.

A big reason to delay sex is an unwanted marriage. I wish you could see my clients, people who even after fifteen years of marriage have never come to grips with the fact that they didn't really want to marry this person but were "forced" to because of an unexpected pregnancy or "false feelings" generated by premarital sex. Premarital sexual activity doesn't prepare you for a good marriage—it usually tricks you into a bad marriage.

Sexually transmitted diseases—as well as the even more serious problems that result from having them, such as cervical cancer—are another big reason to abstain. We'll deal with this topic thoroughly in the next chapter, so for now it's sufficient merely to mention it.

Many experts who talk about "safe sex" fail to mention the

frequent number of "flashbacks" that can occur. Sexual flashbacks are almost like those resulting from hallucinogenic drugs–they seemingly come and go at will, often at the worst possible time. A married woman might be very engaged with her husband, enjoying the throes of sexual passion, and suddenly she can't get Ralph or Fred or John–earlier sexual partners–out of her mind.

The first time this happens can be extremely upsetting. If these flashbacks become regular occurrences, the sexual relationship between this woman and her husband will suffer greatly.

Be Chaste Yourself

Dad, if you want your son to stay chaste before marriage and he finds your stash of *Playboy* magazines, you're fooling yourself if you think he'll listen to your words about saving sex for marriage. "If sex is just about marriage," he'll rightly ask, "why does my dad like to look at pictures of naked women he's not married to?"

If you're a single parent, keep in mind that what's good for your children is good for the parent. I know that many single women with teenage children are reading this book. You've helped steer your kids through close calls with drugs and alcohol. You've helped them deal with an absent parent and the pain of a divorce. Maybe you're a single mom because you've never been married, and your teen is the result of an out-of-wedlock birth. You're reading this book to figure out how to keep your daughter from making the same mistake you made.

Please listen to me. In many ways you are almost as fragile as your teenagers. You've been burned in life, hurt by men, and never had the stability you wanted. It is especially important for you to stay out of bed. Absolutely do not invite your male friends to spend the night, even though you will be sorely tempted to do so.

If you really want to find somebody who is unique, someone who is going to come into your life and accept the kids you have, just think for a few moments about how special this guy has to be. In a world where multimillionaire athletes run out on their own children, you want to find a man who will take responsibility for kids who aren't even his! If you find a man with this kind of character, he won't be the type who will pressure you to have sex or threaten to leave if you refuse to go to bed with him.

You're worth waiting for. Your job is to be different from everybody else who uses sex to cover up pain, which only increases their hurt. Now that you're in your thirties and not your teens, I hope you have the maturity to walk slowly and not give in on the first or second date—or any date before your wedding night.

In fact, though your teenagers are undeniably more vulnerable without a live-at-home dad, you can use your own situation as a teaching moment. Imagine the power behind a conversation that goes like this:

"Honey, I know it's hard for you to see me as a sexual being, but I have the same struggles you do. I know you see John around, and sometimes you say things that make me think you wish he would go away. But I really like him. He's not like the others. He really values me, and that means he doesn't pressure me to sleep with him. We've gone seven months now, and there's been no sex between us, absolutely none. You're old enough to understand what I'm about to tell you—that's not because of a lack of desire. Frankly I crave the close intimate relationship that comes from being physically close to a man. But I know it's best for me to wait. John seems committed to that as well, so guess where my respect for John is? That's right—it couldn't be any higher."

I can't tell you how powerful a conversation like this could be in helping your teenagers to choose abstinence—but you've got to live it first.

If All Else Fails, Get Gross

In many of my books I talk about the influence of "shock power." Sometimes to get our kids' attention, we really have to say something that shocks them. I believe the pressure for sexual activity is so strong today that this is one area where shock power can be of enormous value.

For example, in the next chapter we will look at a chart (page 192) that shows how dangerous it becomes to have numerous sexual partners because people who do are exposing themselves not just to those partners but also to all of *the partners'* partners. I might show the chart to my daughter or client and say, "Do you realize, Michelle, that if you have sex with twelve people, each of whom has had sex with twelve people, that's like putting 4,095 penises inside your body—one at a time?"

Of course that's gross and vile, but it's shocking. And it's true. I can promise you that a young woman will remember it.

Now that you've read this section, I want you to go back with a little file card and write down the reasons for abstinence and the other issues you need to discuss with your adolescents. Have you addressed all of them in the past year? You can't discuss them all at once, of course, but begin looking for ways to complete your children's sexual education.

What If They're *Already* Sexually Active?

So what do you do if you haven't had these talks and you discover birth-control pills in your daughter's dresser drawer? I know some of you think it's a great idea to put your daughter on the pill. I'm saddened by the number of parents who find out their daughter is sexually active and take her to the physician in a resigned manner, getting a prescription for the pill. Personally I think that's *totally* irresponsible on your part as a parent. In my opinion that's granting license to your teenager and is absolutely wrong.

So if you do find evidence of sexual activity, first I recommend you get the teen away from the house and alone, perhaps for a dinner. Then I would have a conversation that went something like this:

"Honey, I don't know how to say this except to come right out with it. Your mom was putting away some of your clothes and found birth-control pills in your top drawer. I suppose right this second you're feeling very uncomfortable that we know you've gone behind our backs to get these pills. Doing that says something about your lifestyle that is very frightening to me, and here are the reasons why.

"Assuming that you're having sex with Brendan, there are a couple things you should know. The pill doesn't protect you from any sexually transmitted diseases. If Brendan has had sex with other people, you're exposing yourself to all their diseases too. In addition to catching a disease that may be with you for the rest of your life, you could get pregnant. If you carry the baby to term, you will be in for a long hard journey, not to mention a baby. If you choose to abort the baby, you will feel tremendous guilt. If the pregnancy leads to a premature marriage, you may regret it for the rest of your life.

"Having sex before you get married is a great way to cripple your sexual satisfaction after you get married. Emotionally and physically, women who have been sexually active prior to marriage or with more than one man usually have more difficulties to overcome.

"For all these reasons, I'm disappointed that you've decided to become sexually active. I think it's wrong and dangerous. While I realize I don't have any control over how you choose to live your life, I feel that, as your father, I have a responsibility to point out to you how destructive your current decisions may be."

Depending on the situation, I might leave it at that. While this may shock some of you, it goes back to not being able to control your adolescent. In case you're still suffering from a severe case of naïveté, let me inform you as a counselor that if two teens are determined to have sex, they're going to have sex. You can load them down with all kinds of rules: "I want you home fifteen minutes after the football game ends—and I'll be listening on the radio for when it ends," but how do you know they're even going to the game? One day in my counseling office a ninth-grade kid confessed that he and his girlfriend had had sex in the laundry room while both parents were at home!

Trying to control kids at this age is a losing game, but don't sell your opinion short. Your thoughts matter more than you realize. Unfortunately some kids (and adults!) are determined to learn the hard way. If your adolescents are bent on taking this road, there is little, unfortunately, that you can do to stop them. All parents want their kids to learn the "easy" way, but kids have minds of their own.

Now that we've talked about sex in general, let's get more specific in the next chapter, where we'll talk about a few sex-related issues of which every modern parent needs to be aware.

Remember:

- Many adolescents are sexually active.
- Teenagers need more than just information; they need their parents' love, understanding, and commitment to get involved in their lives.
- Start early in talking with your children about sex.
- Tell your teens that sex is very good—when it occurs between a husband and wife.
- Your kids need you to be frank, honest, open, affirming, and noncondemning.
- Abstinence is a hard choice for teens today; help them choose purity.
- The best model for healthy sexual relationships is the one your children see in you.
- If your children are already sexually active, talk to them about the consequences.

13

The Seamy Side of Sex

I WAS COUNSELING A fourteen-year-old boy, giving him the typical stuff on sex: "Listen," I said, "it's really important to wait. Besides, girls don't like to be poked and grabbed. Don't make a jerk of yourself like so many young kids do. Be different. Be special."

This young man listened very patiently and almost reverently. I finished my spiel and asked, "Well, do you understand what I'm talking about?"

"Yeah."

"Do you see things like this taking place at your school?"

"Yeah."

"Do you have any questions you'd like to ask me?"

"Yeah."

"What is it?"

"Dr. Leman, what do you do when your girlfriend [who was thirteen, by the way] puts her hand under your shorts and grabs your thing?"

When I tell this story at seminars, you should see the response. I see half the moms with their mouths dropped wide open. A few of the dads, quite frankly, are secretly thinking, *All right! I wish that had happened to me in junior high!*

The story never fails to elicit mixed emotions as it shows just
how much the world has changed and just how great a struggle
our adolescents face as they seek to live a sexually pure life.

If we're going to get anywhere in solving these types of problems with families, we've got to talk turkey; that is, we've got to
be blunt, honest, and forthright. You already know that. That's
why you're taking the time to read this book and why I hope
you'll take the time to engage your teens in talk that will be
even more difficult than what we've already addressed.

"Well, Dr. Leman, what could be more difficult than talking
to your kid about sex?"

Try this: Get even more specific. Talk to your son about masturbation. Talk to your daughter about genital herpes.

See what I mean?

I know you can do it. You've gotten this far, having plowed
your way through one difficult chapter, and many of you are
secretly pining for a break. "Fine. Let's go shopping. Let's see
if there's a game on television. Isn't it time for the six o'clock
news?"

Unfortunately the stakes are too high for us to stop with what
we've already discussed. The things we are going to address in
this chapter will affect your children and grandchildren. Because
the stakes are so high—in some cases, the issues are literally about
life and death—we have to keep going.

As we've already said, these are not easy subjects to discuss,
but I've discovered something curious in my seminars. When
I give adults permission to talk about sex, it takes them a while
to get going, but once they're heated up, I can't shut them up!
Pretty soon couples start raising their hands and asking questions
in front of hundreds or even thousands of people—questions that
they never would have dreamed of asking before the seminar.

The same thing can happen between you and your kids. It may
take a while to get warmed up, but once you develop an open
relationship (remember, it's not about rules or standards—

parenting adolescents is all about building the right kind of relationship), your teens will begin sharing some of their fears, hopes, and even failures. They may initially moan to themselves, *I can't believe I'm having this conversation with my parents!* but eventually they'll be so very glad they have parents who love them so much they are willing to deal with the most sensitive issues in life.

So let's begin. First topic: masturbation, or what I like to refer to as the great exploration.

The Great Exploration

I hope this doesn't shock too many of you, but please allow me to be blunt: your son (and very likely your daughter) is masturbating. Studies show that 96 percent of boys masturbate, and I'm personally convinced that the other 4 percent aren't telling the truth! There appears to be a growing number of young women who are also engaging in this, er, extracurricular activity. Masturbation is one way adolescents can safely relieve their sexual pressures—which are very high, by the way.

As a former adolescent myself, I can't tell you how shocking it is to wake up one night from the most explicit sexual dream you can imagine and realize you've had your first nocturnal emission. This is something that every boy will experience, but almost none will be prepared for it. As a parent you can't avoid this issue of sexual maturation. If a young boy doesn't masturbate on a regular basis, then he is going to have nocturnal emissions. It's one or the other. This is a very natural way for the body to rid itself of the extra semen that accumulates in the young male.

I've spoken with young men—often from very religious backgrounds—who have enormous guilt because they were not prepared by their parents for the onslaught of this experience. They assume they "caused" the dream and may sometimes even consider what happened to be "sinful." They'll try to hide their dirty laundry and go through all sorts of shenanigans to gain some type of privacy and respect.

It's important for us to realize that kids are going to have sexual thoughts during adolescence. This usually will involve some fantasizing, and in the vast majority of cases, some masturbation as well. Parents, be forewarned: You need to allow more privacy for your kids during this period of adolescence.

Although parents in many circles have made masturbation a controversy, I personally don't feel that it's a big deal. As a psychologist, I see masturbation as a normal and harmless part of every person's development—unless it contributes to an unhealthy thought life and feelings of guilt or lust.

Of course we want our boys to live an ethical life. *What moms in particular need to realize is that an ethical life doesn't mean an asexual life.* Nocturnal emissions must be a biological necessity; otherwise, they wouldn't occur. I would put normal patterns of masturbation in this same category.

One of the more healthy things you can do is to make sure your son understands that you are fully aware of how difficult it is these days to maintain sexual purity. For instance, you can tell him, "You know, three hundred years ago you would have married at about your age. Your parents would have picked out a nice young woman for you. But today you've still got a good ten or fifteen years before you'll be financially ready to take on the responsibility of a family, so you need to learn how to control your sexual urges. The best way to do that is by not feeding them. Looking at inappropriate pictures will make you *more* sexually hungry, not less. You'll be satisfied for a little bit, but then you'll want to see even more pictures. The only place that road leads is frustration and anger."

Now, please, listen to this: *The worst thing you can do for your boy at this age is to induce guilt in him for becoming a sexual being.* Masturbation doesn't lead to sexual neurosis, *but false guilt about it can.* In this regard, some of the boys in very religious homes can have a more difficult time than boys from more laid-back homes. Dr. Archibald Hart, a leading psychologist who has counseled numerous male pastors and leaders, warns, "Male sexuality . . . goes wrong whenever early development and the long period of expected abstinence are filled with guilt-producing condemnation. There is a healthy form of guilt we must all learn, but false, neurotic guilt, on the other hand, doesn't stop bad sexual behavior; it only makes matters worse. It's hard enough for the average boy to fight a battle with raging hormones from age twelve until age twenty-five. What is he to do with the guilt created by taboos imposed by insecure or insensitive parents who know how to condemn but who can't teach the ABCs of forgiveness?"

Dr. Hart goes on to say, "Many, many fine moral and good men are haunted by feelings of lust, obsessions about sex, and compulsions to masturbate. This began with extreme feelings of guilt and shame generated during their teenage years. . . . Their obsessions and compulsions never subside, even after years of happy and sexually satisfying marriage. Only hard, dedicated work can remove them. The challenge before us is how to teach sexual self-control without creating neurotic guilt."[1]

Instead of dodging this touchy issue, tackle it head-on. For instance, as you talk about masturbation with your young son, add, "Sex is certainly a wonderful thing, but because we want you to be a responsible young man, you have a few guidelines to follow to make sure sex is something you enjoy rather than something that harms you.

"For instance, in this house, we don't allow pornography. Looking at those pictures isn't appropriate. Of course you're curious about what a woman's body looks like, and we have some books that will show you what a naked woman looks like. But the pictures from dirty magazines display women in a way that is not appropriate.

"Also, the Bible says we shouldn't *imagine* doing anything that wouldn't be right to actually do. You need to learn how to control your thoughts so that while you feel good doing something, you don't get caught up in imagining something that would be wrong."

Along with these guidelines, provide other protection. To help keep masturbation under control, kids need to avoid sexually stimulating movies, television programs, explicit music lyrics or videos, and the like. They should also be engaged in other outlets—athletics, strenuous work, and enjoyable hobbies.

Problem Pregnancies

"You wanted to get pregnant, didn't you?" I asked Jennifer. The young woman finally nodded her head yes.

I was the first person to whom she had admitted the truth.

Intentional pregnancies are something that many parents simply cannot understand. I've found—and research has corroborated my beliefs in this area—that many young women who feel alienated and unloved by the significant others in their lives (parents and family) might purposefully get pregnant to have someone who will really "love" them.

Of course, we adults know this is backward. Babies *take* a lot of love rather than give a lot of love, but young adolescents don't realize that. The fantasy of having their own little baby sounds wonderfully attractive to young teenagers who feel that life has dealt them an unfair hand of one kind or another. It's only after young adolescents have given birth to a child that they begin to realize the awesome responsibility they have incurred by choosing to get pregnant. Even though it's a common assumption that young men are always looking for young women to score on, many young women are careful about the men with whom they have sex.

Other girls get pregnant from "trying" to be good. I've seen these young girls when they and their well-meaning parents come into my office, everyone crying over the pregnancy. Usually the young woman was brought up with traditional

Judeo-Christian values and never even thought about birth control because she wouldn't think of planning on doing anything sinful. But when she and her boyfriend's passion got out of hand, they had intercourse, and she became pregnant.

I recall one young woman, sixteen years old, who became sexually active with her eighteen-year-old boyfriend. Although the young man wanted to purchase some condoms ahead of time, the girl wouldn't let him. Buying a condom would be an admission, in her mind, that she was "choosing" to be sexually active. Even though she and her boyfriend were regularly sleeping together, she was living in a fantasy world, believing that every occurrence happened by accident. Her fantasy became a nightmare after she discovered that her period was three weeks late.

Most often I find that the reason so many teenagers experience out-of-wedlock pregnancies is because most of them simply don't live very structured or planned lives. To them, the future is next Friday. In the process of not taking the time to think about what their physical and sexual limits are in dating relationships, many teenagers find themselves in situations where "one thing led to another." In the height of passion it's very difficult and cumbersome to take time out to use contraceptives of any kind. Teenagers get so caught up in the fantasy of having sex that they don't want any interruptions, even that of protecting themselves from pregnancy. Besides, have you ever seen a movie where, at the height of a titillating love scene, the young lovers stop to use a contraceptive? It just doesn't seem like a romantic thing to do.

Fortunately there's some good news in this regard. According to the Centers for Disease Control, the birth rate for teenagers declined 20 percent between 1991 and 1999. The drop occurred in all age levels, from young teens ages fifteen to seventeen to the youngest group, ages ten to fourteen.[2]

Lest we get complacent, however, let's remember that there are still approximately one million pregnancies that occur annually among American teenagers who are fifteen to nineteen years old. Teen pregnancy rates are still much higher in the United States than in similar developed countries. For example, our teen pregnancy rate is twice as high as that of England and Canada, and nine times as high as that of the Netherlands and Japan.[3]

The social and individual cost of early childbearing is high for both mother and child. Babies of adolescents are far more likely to be poor, and their parents are far more likely to drop out of high school.[4] Although young women may hope their babies bring love and attention, mothers are far more likely to find that having a baby so young brings innumerable and seemingly unending challenges.

I can't say this often enough: Parents need to be involved. We can't expect our adolescents to escape premarital sexuality—and an adolescent pregnancy—if they are left to fend for themselves. They need training, a listening ear, and an active, involved parent. As a therapist I know firsthand that many of our teenagers feel alienated and unloved by their families. Going through the turbulent adolescent years with little perceived love or security in their lives, many teenage girls essentially choose to get pregnant out of a desperate craving to be loved.

The cycle perpetuates itself in a home where the pregnant teenager chooses to keep her baby rather than placing the child for adoption. The overwhelming majority of teen mothers who give birth opt to raise their children themselves. This is unfortunate because babies need two mature adult parents. In virtually every circumstance the best thing for the child is to be adopted into a stable, two-parent home. Teens need to be challenged to think less of themselves and more of their babies.

Of course, pregnancy is by no means the only danger of premarital adolescent sexuality.

What Sex Leaves Behind

If the thought that your adolescents may be involved in an unwanted pregnancy doesn't scare you, this should: Each year, approximately 3 million teens (about one in four sexually experienced teens) acquire a sexually transmitted disease (STD). HIV, the virus that causes AIDS, is the sixth leading cause of death among persons age fifteen to twenty-four years in the United States.[5]

Among the grossest things I've ever seen were the herpes sores a young client showed me. She was wearing shorts, and she pulled them back just a little to reveal the most unsightly sores you could imagine running down the inside of her thighs. Did you know that herpes can run down your legs like that? I didn't. The saddest part is, because of one sexual encounter as an adolescent, she may have to live with these recurring sores for the rest of her life.

Think of it this way: Jack and Jill are doing it on the back side of the hill. Why? They're in *Love!* Not just "love," but *Love* that has never before been experienced in all of human history, a unique human passion discovered only by these two, so the rules don't apply to them.

Unfortunately STDs do.

You see, at seventeen, Jack has had six sexual partners. The first girl he had sex with was fifteen, and she had already had sex with four other boys. The second girl Jack had sex with was fourteen; she had just had sex with two other boys before Jack. When Jack was fifteen, he met Susie, who already had had sex with eight other guys. At sixteen, Jack scored "big," having sex with Lucy (five previous partners), Amy (three previous partners), and Alicia (two previous partners).

Let's do the math: Do you think it's possible that any of the six girls' twenty-four previous partners just "may" have been carrying around some little virus? Jill isn't just having sex with Jack, and she's not just having sex with Jack's six previous partners.

Her body is also being exposed to the twenty-four partners of those partners.

Dr. C. Everett Koop, former surgeon general of the United States, warns, "When you have sex with someone, you are having sex with everyone they have had sex with for the last ten years, and everyone their partners have had sex with for the last ten years."

Consider the following chart that shows how many sexual partners a person (X) might be exposed to if each partner has the same number of sexual partners.[6] With each new partner the risk of exposure to STDs increases exponentially:

Number of X's Partners	Number of Sexual Partners X Is Exposed To
1	1
2	3
3	7
4	15
5	31
6	63
7	127
8	255
9	511
10	1023
11	2047
12	4095

Don't let a relatively small number of sexual partners create a false sense of security, however. In a *single act* of unprotected sex with an infected partner, a teenage female has a 1 percent risk of acquiring HIV, a 30 percent risk of getting genital herpes, and a 50 percent chance of contracting gonorrhea.[7]

Unfortunately it's not enough to steer our kids clear of physical contact; now we have to help them navigate the asteroid-laden skies of cyberspace as well!

Sex of the Cyber Kind

Mom and Dad, would you let pornography come home with your teens? Would you allow your son to leave "skin" magazines lying out in the open in the family room?

"Of course not," most of you would say.

I've got news for you. Pornography is in your home right now. Turn on the computer, and plug in some "innocent" sounding words. Just for fun, I went to yahoo.com, one of the most popular search sites on the net, and typed in the word *love*. The first four responses were:

1. Hewitt, Jennifer Love
2. Love and Sex
3. Kama Sutra: A Tale of Love
4. The Incredibly True Adventure of Two Girls in Love

In my day a boy had to go out of his way to get hold of pornographic material. Today it comes right into most homes. In May of 2000, the United States Supreme Court overturned a federal law that required pornographic cable TV channels to fully scramble or otherwise block transmission of those channels between the hours of six o'clock in the morning and ten o'clock at night. This seems like such a small and reasonable restriction, but the court somehow found it "unconstitutionally overbroad."

One of the dangers for young girls was revealed when a government-financed survey found that one in five adolescents and teens who regularly socialize on the Internet have encountered a stranger who wanted "cybersex."[8] The good news is that 75 percent of these teens brushed off the advances. But parents need to be aware of what their children may encounter while spending time in "chat rooms" and surfing the Internet.

If your teenagers get caught in this web, it could ruin them vocationally. Occasionally I've had to help couples through this troublesome addiction. Jerry had started a successful business that was profitable in its second year and showed increasing profits for an additional three years. Imagine his wife's surprise when she discovered that business—and their income—dropped by almost 75 percent a few years later.

It turns out that Jerry was spending up to *eight hours a day* surfing pornographic Web sites. He lost all discipline, and his business tanked. All but the most urgent items were ignored while he looked for yet another picture of some well-endowed woman.

Cybersex addiction is a growing problem that parents of adolescents need to become familiar with, as these addictions often start in a person's teenage years. There is now a center for on-line addiction that specializes in treating people with just this problem.[9]

In previous generations there was a stigma (as well as an age limit) attached to actually entering an adult bookstore. The seeming anonymity of the Web has removed a tremendous psychological barrier, unleashing a torrent of new cybersex addicts.

In her book *Caught in the Net: How to Recognize the Signs of Internet Addiction,* Dr. Kimberly Young offers several warning signs that may indicate signs of a cybersex addiction.[10]

A change in sleep patterns. An addiction is a condition marked by a person's loss of control. Sleep is never as enticing as feeding the addiction, so a cybersex addict is likely to stay up late surfing the Web. My advice is that teens should not have unrestricted access to the Internet. Keep the family computer in a place that is public and that discourages secretive viewing.

A demand for privacy. If your teens suddenly act defensive or quickly turn off the screen as soon as you walk into the room, they may be looking at something they don't want you to know about. There's no shame in checking out sports scores, and teens aren't likely to get agitated if you catch them reviewing a report on botany.

Stanford University's Dr. Al Cooper conducted a survey of

more than 9,000 visitors to on-line, sex-related sites. He found that 72 percent of the men and 62 percent of the women kept secret just how much time they spent on-line for sexual pursuits. If your children act with undue defensiveness or anger when you walk up behind them on the computer, you have reason to be suspicious.

And please, don't assume that only boys are at risk here. A woman recently wrote to Ann Landers, concerned that her twelve-year-old niece was using her computer to access pornographic Web sites. The woman thought the young girl just wanted to play some harmless games, so she let her use the computer unattended. The next time the woman logged on, however, she was able to check the history of the sites her niece had visited—and the aunt was appalled.

The saddest thing of all is a case that is not unusual anymore: an overweight sixteen-year-old girl discovered a thirty-one-year-old "soul mate" on-line, and the teen actually ran away from home to meet him. While boys may gravitate toward immediate satisfaction (that can lead to masturbation), girls often develop relationships that may be entirely inappropriate. You need to know what your children are doing on-line—what sites they are visiting, and with whom they are "chatting."

To accomplish this, it is essential that you keep computers with modem hookups out of your kids' rooms! An Internet-accessible computer should be kept in a central place that doesn't afford much privacy.

Ignoring other responsibilities. Is your adolescents' schoolwork taking a nosedive? Are they leaving their chores undone? Do they wake up later and later in the morning, and begin to miss previously favored activities, like basketball practice or skating lessons? While many factors could contribute to this behavior, be aware that these may also be indicators that something else has captured their affection—cybersex.

Evidence of lying. Addiction always leads to lying, and the deceit inevitably stretches out to eventually become a way of life. First, cybersex addicts will lie about what they're looking at. Second, if caught, they'll try to explain away the clear evidence. They'll say they were doing a report on pornography and that's why they had to visit the "Hot Vixens" Web site.

A young woman who has found a new "friend" on-line may begin making excuses to be out of the house. Are you sure she's really spending the night with her friend, or is she on a bus to meet the guy she met on-line?

Money comes into play here, as well. Many pornographic sites require credit cards, but these companies mask the charges with innocuous sounding names: "Franklin Entertainment" or "CSS On-line Services."[11] If you notice any charges that don't seem familiar to you, check them out.

Personality changes. Kimberly Young notes that people are often surprised to see how much cybersex addicts' moods and behaviors change once the Internet engulfs them. A once warm and sensitive person can become cold and withdrawn. Or a formerly lighthearted person can turn quiet and brooding.

Of course, some personality changes are part of adolescence, but if you notice this along with any other hints, it's time to do some research of your own.

Less interest in family. Again, we have to be careful here, as adolescents are notorious for trying to skip out on family activities to spend time with their peers, but be aware that any addiction is like a black hole for time, money, and emotional energy. Everything else must suffer and bend to meet the needs of the ever-growing addiction. If teens who were formerly involved with the family suddenly become surly whenever they have to spend time together, you have reason to find out why.

To counteract the growing threat of Internet pornography, consider switching to a family-friendly Internet service provider such as Integrity On-line, which filters out inappropriate sites. Of course, many software programs do the same thing.[12] When selecting one, just make sure that you know more about how the program works than your adolescents do!

Shacking Up

Another issue that is becoming more and more of a problem is adolescents who not only become sexually active but also actually move in together. Usually the adolescents who do this are older, though occasionally a younger teen might run off with an older person.

Kay and John are a typical example of the couples I've seen in my private practice more often than I'd like to admit. They came to me after being married for just six months, but by that time they had lived together for almost two years. Not surprisingly the day after they got married, things began to disintegrate. All of a sudden they were confronted with problems that never existed when they were living together: increased quarreling, decreased sexual intimacy, and ongoing power struggles. They were legitimately confused and puzzled when they came for marital therapy. Why did getting married seemingly make things *worse?*

Like thousands of other couples, John and Kay made a serious judgment error. They bought the lie that living together was a foolproof way to test whether or not they were compatible for marriage. It's a sad but common misconception. According to the U.S. Bureau of the Census, between 1960 and 1997 the number of cohabiting couples went from fewer than 500,000 to 4 million, an 800 percent increase.[13] Unfortunately more than 50 percent of marriages are now preceded by cohabitation.[14]

A recent Penn State study found that couples who live together before getting married have poorer communication skills when trying to solve problems than those who didn't cohabit before they were married. Study coauthor Catherine Cohan suggests that cohabitants "may have less invested in the relationship, leading them not to try to develop their skills."[15]

In fact, the research now shows that cohabitation actually

cripples a marriage's chance for success rather than vice versa. Researchers David Popenoe and Barbara Dafoe Whitehead point out that only one-sixth of cohabiting relationships last three years, and only one in ten last five years or more.[16] Worse, every one of these failed, cohabiting relationships makes people a little less fit to enjoy a lifelong, satisfying marriage. Rather than prepare couples for marriage, cohabiting prepares them to break up. Without the deeper commitment of marriage, couples train themselves to "run" from relational problems rather than work to solve them.

At the risk of sounding archaic, I need to point out that this is especially true for women. I know we aren't supposed to see differences between men and women these days, but only someone who has never counseled more than two people could seriously believe that. Throughout my practice, I've been amazed at how easily men are able to separate the "physical" from the "emotional." For instance, I've had several husbands tell me—without any hint of irony or any awareness of the absurdity of what they were saying—that they've been "good husbands" and have had sex with only five, six, or eight other women during their marriage! For whatever reason, men seem to be able to distinguish between physical relationships and emotional relationships more easily than women do. The fact remains that women, more so than men, tend to carry the emotional scars of a relationship that doesn't last.

For some women, guilt associated with living together before marriage is an added burden that they must carry throughout life. Even those who seemingly have been able to intellectualize their "living arrangements" and appear to reject their parents' values and religious instruction cannot shake guilty feelings. Here's the kicker: this guilt often remains *even if the woman marries the man with whom she has lived.* Sometimes it even makes her feel more guilty! It really is a rare individual who can reject family values and live a lifestyle contrary to those values without suffering from a certain amount of guilt.

If my nineteen-year-old adolescent son (or daughter) were determined to live with someone while at college, and I was paying his tuition, the checks would stop immediately. If he is old enough to make that decision, he's old enough to take care of himself. I would say something like this:

"Listen, I wish you guys the best, but if you insist on playing husband and wife, you can do it on your own dime."

"But, Dad," Junior would protest, "how can I afford it?"

"I don't think you can," I would admit. "I guess you'll have to get jobs and go to community college."

Honestly, I can't stop them from living together. I would tell them I'm disappointed, that I think they're making a big mistake. Then I would let them pay the price—but at that point that's all I can do. Legally, they're adults.

If your teenagers are considering a live-in relationship, I urge you to have them read my book *The Birth Order Connection*. It should open their eyes to what really makes a good marital match.

Does It Really Matter?

While some of you are agreeing with almost everything I've just said, others of you are thinking I'm taking this premarital sex stuff way too seriously. Does it really matter whether we raise kids who remain virgins until they are married?

Before you dismiss my thoughts as old-fashioned, I want to introduce you to Chuck, a former client who agreed to tell his story in hopes that someone else might be helped by his experiences.

"Premarital sex is something I would never have dreamed I'd be talking to anyone about because as I was going through school, sex—along with alcohol and dope—was the thing to do. You weren't cool if you hadn't been laid in a while. I remember how embarrassed I'd be when I told my friends I hadn't been laid by a certain girl I went out with. It just wasn't cool. It wasn't really until I'd grown up a little bit that I found out just what kind of adverse effect premarital sex has. Especially for the woman. I hate to say that; I hate to sound biased, but especially for the woman.

"I have a good friend who shared how she and her boyfriend were madly in love. They just knew they were the right ones for each other. They got into it hot and heavy; she said she gave herself to him, literally, because in sex the two really do become one. Premarital sex puts a strain on a relationship because the relationship then becomes just physical. Instead of meeting and talking, sharing your day, going to a movie, just enjoying being with each other, you get together, have sex, and leave. You meet just to fulfill your needs, you might say.

"Anyhow, this friend and her boyfriend, after a couple months, found out that they weren't right for each other after all, that they weren't really meant to get married. She's twenty-one years old, a college graduate, and a beautiful girl. As she told me about this, I could see in her eyes the hurt she had gone through. She said she would wake up in the morning and vomit blood because she was so upset. She had given herself to somebody who turned out to be the wrong person, and she couldn't get back what she lost. It's kind of like giving someone a million dollars and later finding out you gave it to the wrong person, but now he's gone—and so is your money. Gone for good. You don't have it anymore, and the person who should have had it will now never get it.

"I recently started going out with a woman whom I knew a few years ago. One thing I admired back then, really liked and respected about her, was that she wasn't messing around with anybody. Even when I was messing around with drugs and alcohol, I still had a high ideal of what I wanted in a woman, and this person was my kind of woman because she didn't give in to guys. Well, after I became a Christian and changed my lifestyle, this woman came back into my life. We started going out to dinner and talking and sharing our lives. It was just beautiful. She was just as lovely as she was the day I first met her.

"One day she shared some experiences she was struggling with. She said that she had had sex with this guy. She looked at me and said, 'Chuck, if there is some way I could just turn back the hands of time. . . .' I don't think the guy was worried about it, but I guarantee you my friend was. He had given her the ultimatum that 'if you love me you will.' She felt she loved him, so she gave in. She never felt right about it, and it really had a traumatic psychological effect on her.

"Then, when we were having dinner one night, she told me about another guy. She thought she was going to marry him and lived with him for two years while she went through college. I can't tell you what her telling me that did to me. It was like a slap in the face. Here was this woman I thought was so special, that I had such high regard for, telling me that she lived with somebody for two years. For some reason that just didn't set right with me. I had hoped that the woman I would fall in love with and marry would share all the little deep secrets of her mind, her feelings, and her philosophy with just me. I think when you're lying in bed with different people all of the time, it's kind of hard to know who's special and who's not. Don't get me wrong. She wasn't having sex with a lot of different people. But living two years with a guy, a lot of things can happen between them.

"But when I talked with Dr. Leman about this, he explained to me that I had taken away a lot of those special things from girls I had sex with in high school. That really hit me. Some of those young women know in the back of their minds that they will have to share our experiences with the man they fall in love with. I can imagine how those men are going to feel. I felt it once, but I might have caused it ten times.

"I know one woman who told me she doesn't hold hands or kiss or anything on a date. By today's standards that's kind of hard to believe. She's a beautiful college woman, but she doesn't want to get trapped in any kind of a relationship until she gets married. She wants to keep all her dates on a friendship basis. I think that's neat."

Let me tell you, premarital sex changes people. It makes them harder, more vulnerable, and less able to make a wise choice when it comes time to get married. If your adolescents engage in premarital sex, it will also make them less attractive to the type of spouse who is of high character and who will remain faithful throughout their entire marriage.

Ann, age thirty-three, came to me on referral from her gynecologist. She was becoming more and more distressed because of "flashbacks" during intercourse with her husband, and she asked her doctor to refer her to a psychologist who could help her deal with this issue. I mentioned flashbacks earlier in the book, but I want to get even more explicit here so you can see exactly what I mean.

Ann and Michael were married when she was twenty-six. Michael walked into Ann's life after she graduated from college, and he was what she had always wanted in a man. As a college student, Ann had numerous sexual encounters with a variety of men; none of them mattered to her as much as Michael, but now she couldn't get previous sexual memories out of her mind.

It got so bad that in order for Ann to reach orgasm while having sex with her husband, she had to fantasize about someone else. Ann, naturally, was horrified by this. Michael was a good father to their two children and held down a good job. He was attentive, affectionate, and helpful around the house—a good husband all the way around. But as soon as Ann felt her husband's arms around her, one of her previous lovers would pop into her mind.

"As I look into my husband's eyes, I see Jack or Ron or Steve. I didn't even like Steve! It was a horrible relationship. But thoughts of these men are affecting my desire for Michael. And now Michael and I are having tremendous sexual problems in our marriage."

Although it has become vogue to throw out the old-fashioned tradition of remaining a virgin until marriage, there certainly are many practical reasons for abstaining until then. Flashbacks, although not one of the reasons typically listed for saying no, is yet another one that's worthy of consideration.

Setting Standards

As much as we parents may not like the thought of our children becoming sexually active, the truth is, if they want to have sex, they can—and will. It is not possible to monitor adolescents twenty-four hours a day. They can lie about where they're going. They can cut a few corners and meet their boyfriends or girl-friends while walking home from school. Two teens can find any number of ways to spend time alone.

All of this is to say that it is impera-tive for you to help your children establish standards of their own. It's helpful to acknowledge from the start that your children's standards might be different from yours. I know that sounds dangerous to many of you, but keep in mind—when adolescents are alone, in the backseat of a car late at night, their standards are all that will matter. If you go about this the right way, you'll often find your teens' standards to be very similar to yours. And once your adolescents take ownership of these standards, they are far more likely to live by them.

> It is imperative for you to help your children establish standards of their own.

In chapter 11, the dating chapter, I outlined a possible conver-sation to have when your teenagers first begin to date. You ask them to write out their dating guidelines, and then you discuss those guidelines with your teens. That exercise and the discussions that will result from it will pay big dividends in your adolescents' lives.

But what if you haven't done that? Is it too late now?

If you haven't been discussing guidelines for sexuality, the place to start is with an apology. "Julie, I'm sorry that we haven't discussed this before. I know that sex is something we haven't talked about, but we're going to now." This is the better-late-than-never philosophy. Review chapters 11 and 12 for more help, or read them with your adolescents, and use them as a springboard for further discussion

I'm not suggesting that sexual morality is relative. Certainly there are absolutes, and if you have a faith tradition, I think it's important to call your children to uphold the dictates of their faith. Jews, Christians, and Muslims all oppose premarital sexuality, and this provides an opportunity for your children to learn how to live according to their faith.

> Call your children to uphold the dictates of their faith.

But what I am suggesting is that the time will come when your children must decide for themselves that they will accept your faith and the sexual standards that come along with it. Eventually each one of us must decide what we will do, and won't do, with our bodies. I want you to help your children make a conscious decision, rather than fall into a belief that arises *after* passion has already led them astray.

Your children need to know that once they set these standards, they will feel guilty about breaking them. Also acknowledge to them that there are going to be times they wish they could "indulge." They're going to be tempted, and these temptations are very natural, even universal. But the question is, "Are you going to allow your emotions to control your behavior, or are you going to learn to consciously control your emotions?"

You don't help your children by making it sound "easy." Frankly it's not. Again, I was a virgin when I got married, but it wasn't an easy journey for me by any means. I couldn't wait to have sex, and I don't expect it to be any different for my kids. Even so, every day hundreds of couples get married and experience sex for the first time with each other. This is an ideal worth pursuing. It will give them the best start in life and the greatest chance for a sexually fulfilling marriage.

Remember:

- Masturbation is a normal part of sexual development.
- We can't expect adolescents to escape premarital sexuality—and an adolescent pregnancy—if they are left to fend on their own. We must stay involved.
- Sexual promiscuity increases adolescents' chances of contracting sexually transmitted diseases.
- Keep the computer with Internet access in a place that is public and that discourages secretive viewing.
- Use a filter that blocks access to pornographic Web sites.
- Cohabitation actually *cripples* a marriage's chance for success rather than vice versa.
- Help your adolescents set standards for their dating relationships.

14

Troubled
Teens

EVEN IF YOU ARE good parents, your kids may turn out a little different from what you hoped. You can do everything right but still end up with kids who walk to a troublesome beat. The innate truth is that God made us all different, giving kids the same free choice he gives us as adults. Some kids, in spite of their good nurturing and stable home life, decide they're going to do it their own way.

Unfortunately not only do they pay for it, but others around them are forced to pay for their decisions as well. Toddlers can be noisy, but adolescents can wind up in jail. The potential for real trouble increases exponentially once children reach their teens.

Let's look at some of the more common ways teens can go wrong.

Eating Disorders

Jim and Sharon were caught totally by surprise.

Their first mistake was having such a busy schedule that they couldn't monitor what was going on in their daughter Annie's life. Their family ate so few meals together that they didn't realize how little Annie was eating—sometimes not much more than a carrot and a piece of lettuce. When Annie said she had "already eaten," they took her at her word. She so frequently said she was going to "eat later, at a friend's house," that it never occurred to Jim and Sharon that their sixteen-year-old was slowly starving herself.

The ordeal started for the stupidest of reasons. Teenagers can be cruel, and once during gym class, Annie thought she heard somebody refer to the back of her legs as "cottage cheese."

Those words hit a trigger, and Annie slipped into the spider-web of anorexia nervosa, an eating disorder that, if not diagnosed and treated, can eventually be fatal as the young woman literally starves herself to death.

In today's appearance-obsessed world, parents of adolescents need to become sensitive to symptoms of eating disorders. Anorexia nervosa involves dieting or not eating sufficiently, with the result that people's body weight drops 15 percent or more below the standard guidelines. Even when these people look frightfully thin, they may continue to starve themselves.

Another disorder is bulimia, or "binge-purge" disorder. This occurs when people habitually binge—perhaps eating an entire half gallon of ice cream or a full box of doughnuts—and then purge by inducing vomiting to get rid of the calories. Some teens will turn to excessive use of laxatives in lieu of vomiting.

Both eating disorders wreak havoc on a developing body. They throw young women's hormones out of whack, bring their menstrual cycles to a complete halt, and stress the heart to the point of death. These eating disorders are also frighteningly prevalent. Vicki Harvey, a clinical psychologist from southern California, writes: "There are more than five million diagnosable anorexics and bulimics in the United States. One percent of teenage girls in the U.S. develop anorexia, and at least one thousand die each year. Up to 5 percent of college women in the U.S. are bulimic. In addition to people actually suffering from anorexia and bulimia, another 20 million Americans demonstrate eating-disordered thinking that could quickly switch to an active disorder."[1]

The theme observed in anorexics is perfectionism. More than 90 percent of all anorexics are young women. It doesn't take much thought to realize that the constant bombardment of "thin is beautiful!" models in magazine ads and within the media in general has increased young women's unrealistic expectations of the perfect body.

What should you be looking out for in your adolescents? Beware of a sudden change in clothing, particularly bulky clothing, which may be used to conceal either weight loss or gain. If you notice a consistent and frequent retreat to a bathroom following the evening meal, find out what's going on behind closed doors. It's fine to eavesdrop in this case!

Excessive and obsessive exercising is another warning sign. When a music reviewer mentioned singer Karen Carpenter's weight, she started practically living on an exercise bicycle to shed pounds. Her quest for the perfect weight eventually cost the young singer her life.

Young teens with food problems may also show signs of concern while they eat—either by dicing their food into the smallest of bites or by just pushing it around on their plates without really eating anything. They may stick their fork into their potatoes, for instance, but bring it back to their mouth without actually having anything of substance on it. This isn't normal behavior, so if you see your teens doing this, seek professional help. The sooner, the better, in this case. The longer a person suffers from either eating disorder, the more difficult it will be to overcome it.

Vicki recommends that "if they talk about their fears of being fat, don't argue with them. And don't get into discussions about what they are doing to their bodies. All the facts in the world do not matter because their perception of themselves distorts reality. Remember that an eating disorder is a symptom that a person feels terrible about him or herself and has little control over [his or] her life. They think nothing they do is good enough, so they resort to the idea that if they could at least get really thin, then they'd be a success at something."[2]

If you're not to argue with them, what do you do? Get them to a professional.[3] You and your teens are going to need help with this one. Harvey points out that "people do not grow out of eating disorders on their own. They are complex and deep rooted and involve deeply painful feelings."[4]

If your adolescents refuse to go with you to seek help, visit a specialist on your own for assistance in getting your teens to come in.

In this area, like all areas, parental example is paramount. Harvey writes that caring parents need to become living examples to their troubled teens. "Avoid diets and preoccupation with thinness and food. Be physically active and enthusiastic about life. Try to evaluate your tendency to affirm others' worth based on performance. Begin demonstrating that it is the person, not [his or her] accomplishments, that is important to you. Admit that you get angry, frustrated, afraid, and needy. Talk about your feelings and emotional and spiritual needs, and model how to take responsibility for them."[5]

You see, Harvey is telling you to do what I've already suggested elsewhere in this book. Be real, be involved, be present, and be active. That'll help you face virtually any challenge your adolescents come across.

Suicide

"In the fall of fourth grade I decided to kill myself."

So begins the story of Rev. David Murphy, a Washington State pastor.[6] "On a Sunday afternoon I silently slipped a butcher knife from the kitchen drawer by the sink and stole down the rickety wooden steps to the basement.

"It was an old-fashioned, unfinished basement, with a sloped drain in the middle of the floor; cobwebs festooned the rough, aged joists overhead. Familiar smells of damp earth and concrete comforted me. I was the only one who spent time there.

"Lifting my T-shirt under the yellow light of a dusty bulb hanging from the ceiling, I studied my own anatomy. Then I placed the point of the long knife just below my ribs on the left side and slowly pulled the knife into the soft skin, which indented around the point.

"With sudden misgiving, I adjusted the angle of the blade. This was important. If the angle were wrong, the knife would not strike the heart. I would be wounded—unconcealably—but not dead. I wasn't afraid of dying, but I was terrified of failing in the attempt; it could call down unimaginable wrath from my parents.

"I wavered, uncertain of my knowledge of anatomy, drawn mainly from my Visible Man, which had been a birthday gift. About a foot tall, his hard plastic body parts could be taken apart and put back together. I was trying to extrapolate from the small plastic heart of the Visible Man to my own heart and the precise vector needed for the knife. I was guessing and knew it, and couldn't bring myself to trust a guess. I lowered the knife, climbed back upstairs, put the knife away, and cried."

The most chilling words are yet to come. After writing this harrowing account, Murphy adds, "Nobody ever found out."

Imagine your adolescents, so fed up with life that they wanted to end it right there, even plotting how to do that, and beginning to carry it out, thrusting the tip of a knife into their skin until it almost punctures—then putting the knife away, *and never telling anyone about it.*

Tragically this happens far more than you might think. Even worse, many teens actually follow through on their attempts. Suicide kills more people each year than homicide or AIDS. There are about 500,000 known suicide attempts on an annual basis, with 30,000 actually succeeding.[7]

According to a report published by the United States surgeon general, the incidence of suicide attempts reaches a peak during the midadolescent years. Suicide is the third leading cause of death among teenagers. The suicide rate for fifteen- to nineteen-year-olds is about six times higher than for ten- to fourteen-year-olds. In the older group, boys are about four times as likely as girls to actually *commit* suicide, while girls are twice as likely to *attempt* suicide.[8]

As Murphy looks back on his near suicide, he remarks, "It's surprising how trivial were the events I nearly let kill me: Annette's rejection; being cut from a basketball team; flunking out of school; being unpopular for a time."

These "trivial" events take on great importance in the adolescent mind, leading many to a desperate "solution." One of the most significant warning signs of a possible suicide attempt includes a major depression.

According to the surgeon general's report, "Depressed children are sad, they lose interest in activities that used to please them, and they criticize themselves and feel that others criticize them. They feel unloved, pessimistic, or even hopeless about the future; they think that life is not worth living, and thoughts of suicide may be present. Depressed children and adolescents are often irritable, and their irritability may lead to aggressive behavior. They are indecisive, have problems concentrating, and may lack energy or motivation; they may neglect their appearance and hygiene; and their normal sleep patterns are disturbed."[9]

The report also points to studies that show that at any given time, between 10 and 15 percent of the child and adolescent population are exhibiting some symptoms of depression. If your children have been depressed before, odds are good (about 20 to 40 percent) that they will experience a relapse within two years. By adulthood, most of the adolescents (70 percent) who have experienced depression will experience it again. One thing is clear: "Children and particularly adolescents who suffer from depression are at much greater risk of committing suicide than are children without depression."

Further adding to the mix are "anxiety symptoms," which, when associated with depression, may include "fears of separation or reluctance to meet people, and somatic symptoms, such as general aches and pains, stomachaches, and headaches."

In the report, researchers speculate that one reason why more girls than boys attempt suicide is that girls "are more socially oriented, more dependent on positive social relationships, and more vulnerable to losses of social relationships than are boys. This would increase their vulnerability to the interpersonal stresses that are common in teenagers."

In general, the report continues, the most significant suicide risk factor among girls is "the presence of major depression, which, in some studies, increases the risk of suicide twelvefold. The next most important risk factor is a previous suicide attempt, which increases the risk approximately threefold. Among boys, a previous suicide attempt is the most potent predictor, increasing the rate over thirtyfold. It is followed by depression (increasing the rate by about twelvefold), disruptive behavior (increasing the rate by twofold), and substance abuse (increasing the rate by just under twofold)."

Following these are "stressful life events," which might include "getting into trouble at school or with a law enforcement agency; a ruptured relationship with a boyfriend or a girlfriend; or a fight among friends. They are rarely a sufficient cause of suicide, but they can be precipitating factors in young people."

Low levels of communication between parents and children also apparently pose a "significant risk factor" for attempted adolescent suicide, as can exposure to "real or fictional accounts of suicide, including media coverage of suicide, such as intensive reporting of the suicide of a celebrity, or the fictional representation of a suicide in a popular movie or TV show. The risk is especially high in the young, and it lasts for several weeks. The suicide of a prominent person reported on television or in the newspaper or exposure to some sympathetic fictional representation of suicide may also tip the balance and make the at-risk individual feel that suicide is a reasonable, acceptable, and in some instances even heroic, decision."[10]

In short, if you suspect your children may be depressed, it's vital that you learn what is going on in their minds. Particularly if they know of people—even famous people on TV—who end their lives, you need to talk with your kids and rebuild the walls of communication. Researchers have found that discussing suicide does not make depressed adolescents more inclined to commit suicide; on the contrary, they will be emotionally relieved by the opportunity to discuss their feelings. The truth is, they are as scared of these feelings as you are!

The sad thing is, by my observation, many teenagers who have taken their lives were actually extremely good students in school and were very highly thought of by others. What matters most is not how others view them but *how they view themselves*. Maybe they felt that they were unworthy or unimportant. They may have grown up in an environment where parents pushed the level of expectation so high that the teenagers were crushed by the weight of high demands. Or perhaps the teens placed these high expectations on themselves.

I know it is downright scary even to think about teenage suicide. Even so, many, perhaps most, of these tragedies could be prevented if parents would dedicate themselves to honest and open communication with their adolescents. Before their children become teenagers, wise parents will plant the seed in their kids' minds that the coming years may be stormy ones. Then, if your teenagers begin to experience some weird, crazy, upsetting feelings and find themselves tempted to withdraw and keep everything inside, that seed you planted years earlier will germinate, grow, and give them strength to ward off some of those feelings of desolation and loneliness. Then the door will once again be open for you and your teenagers to discuss the problems and emotions they are facing.

Most important, if they don't have to face the feelings alone, they have a much better chance of surviving their teenage years intact.

Runaways

I once worked with a fourteen-year-old kid who had older parents, but they were really fine people, as nice as any people you could find. The boy, unfortunately, didn't realize how good he had it. Because his parents were older, he thought his parents were out of it—the strangest and strictest parents God had ever afflicted on any adolescent in the history of the world.

This boy, Jimmy, was the baby of the family and wild enough to make me think he might take off and run. He certainly had no hesitancy in making such threats, frequently taunting his parents with phrases like "I don't have to take this" and "If you don't lighten up, I'm outta here. I'll find somewhere else to live."

Because Jimmy said the same things to me in confidence, I believed him. In fact, I thought it was just a matter of time until he might try to take off on his own.

Accordingly I worked to prepare Jimmy's parents for his eventual running away. "Jimmy's a pretty good kid," I assured them, "but, as you know, he does have a rebellious streak that he's determined to follow. Don't get too worried. Sometimes kids have to fail in order to learn a lesson—and home is a place where kids can learn from their failures. It's a part of life."

I gave Jimmy's mom, Constance, practical advice for how to handle things if Jimmy should take off. For starters, I urged her not to do what most parents do: immediately call the authorities, report that a child is missing, and generally make a big deal about the whole episode.

This might surprise you, but while a lot of kids run away, most don't go anywhere. That is, they never leave town, instead choosing to hide out at a relatively safe place, such as a friend's house. You would think that if a kid practically moved into their house, most parents would notify the teen's parents. I wish I could tell you that's what would happen, but in most cases it doesn't. Rather, the friend's parents just take the kid's words at face value. When he says, "My parents know I'm here," maybe even adding a sob story—"Their marriage is going through some rough times right now, and it's not the best place for me to be"—they believe him and never follow up.

True to my suspicions, Jimmy took off. Constance called me, frantic, scared, and understandably worried. I did my best to calm her down. "Just sit tight; he'll probably make contact with you before too long."

Well, I was wrong on one count. It took three days for contact to be made. The mom was very anxious about the entire situation, but when we did some research and discovered that Jimmy was going to school, we knew he wasn't in any immediate danger.

The thing I was wrong about was that it wasn't Jimmy who made the contact. He sent a representative to offer terms! This representative showed up on a Sunday morning, believe it or not, with a list of demands. Jimmy wanted a pair of his tennis shoes, a rock band T-shirt, and his boom box.

Constance handled it very well. She went and got the stuff and gave it to the kid, without showing any concern, anger, or vindictiveness.

I had a fun time just imagining the conversation between Jimmy and his friend: "Well, what did my mom say?"

"Not much," the rep answers, surprised as anyone. "She said, 'Yes,' 'Okay,' and 'I think that'll do it.' "

"That's it?"

"That's it. That's all she said."

The very next day, having realized his parents weren't pining over his absence, Jimmy returned—though he took a circuitous route. He started walking up and down the sidewalk in front of his house, waiting for his parents to rush out, make a scene, and create some sort of sentimental drama.

The issue here, however, was power, and I had warned Constance and her husband against giving in to Jimmy's fantasies. As Constance watched Jimmy walking up and down the sidewalk, casting glances in the direction of the house, she actually found herself stifling a laugh. Everything was working out exactly as we had planned it.

Finally Jimmy got it through his head that there would be no welcoming committee and that he might wear out his shoes before anybody noticed his return, so he started to walk toward the house. Constance deliberately raced upstairs when she saw Jimmy begin to make his move.

After waiting a good five minutes, Constance casually walked into the kitchen, where Jimmy was sitting, and remembered my words about throwing Jimmy a "curveball." She did it perfectly.

"Where have you been?" Constance asked. "I haven't seen you around for a day or two. Oh, listen honey, if anyone calls, tell them I'll be back in about an hour. I need to go to the mall and pick up some things."

With that she gathered her purse and keys and walked out the door. Let me tell you, Jimmy was about as shocked as they come. He couldn't believe what had just taken place.

For her part, Constance spent what she calls "the longest hour of my life." Of course, she wanted to grab Jimmy, hug him, kiss him, and smother him with love, but she remembered our conversations and wisely refrained.

When she returned from the mall, Jimmy was in his room but soon came down, sheepishly staring at his shoes. He finally ran into Constance's arms and apologized for running away, promising never to do it again. Most important, he lost the weapon he had used against his parents for years. No longer could he strike fear into their hearts by threatening to run away.

This is one of those instances where I believe parents need to allow reality to teach their kids. The fact is, we provide wonderful homes for our children. We can't make them stay in our home, however, and if our kids do leave, they will soon find out that the world at large isn't nearly as accommodating as we are. So if they want to try out life on the outside for a while, let them!

Now, I do make exceptions. You need to know your children and your neighborhood before you make a decision about how to respond. I wouldn't have told Constance to respond the way she did, for instance, if her fourteen-year-old daughter had just run off with a twenty-five-year-old man. We would have had the police on that couple faster than you could dial 911.

In fact, I worked with one family whose fifteen-year-old daughter ran away, only to be found dead the next morning, the victim of a strangler. In some instances running away presents tremendous danger; however, in many cases, the danger is minimal, and parents shouldn't keep running after the kids. Once our children reach a certain age, it is only by voluntary agreement that they live in our homes.

Hate Groups

Hate groups are, sadly, a modern concern with which parents need to become familiar. In many cases, I believe young people join such groups in a desperate attempt to belong. These groups use insecurity and hate as a social bond, which appeals to adolescents whose family bonds have failed. Frequently violent, but not always so, hate groups are extremely damaging to your children's psychological health. We live in a diverse world; the refusal to get along with anybody who is different will lead to a frustrating and unproductive existence.

Because hate groups fall outside the bounds of "political correctness," such groups often resort to symbols to express their membership. If you see these symbols on your teen's skateboard, notebook, or as a tattoo, you have some investigating to do. (You should also become aware of these symbols in case your daughter begins dating one of these guys, or your son begins hanging out with other boys who display these signs.)

Any Nazi sign or corrupted cross (either bent or upside down) is a danger sign. Less well-known symbols to watch out for include a picture of a fist with the letters S-K-I-N written across each knuckle. This is a symbol of racist skinheads, alluding to the Aryan or "white power" fist. If you see a picture of a skull with a patch over one eye, with crossbones beneath it, and the word *WAR* above it, you're looking at the symbol of the White Aryan Resistance, a neo-Nazi skinhead organization that espouses hatred against Jews, blacks, Asians, and virtually any nonwhites.

A spiderweb tattoo, which usually has to be earned either by spending time in jail for committing a racially oriented crime or, in worst-case scenarios, by killing a minority person, is also a sign of involvement in hate groups.

Crossed hammers set on top of various images mark the territory of Hammerskins and the Hammerskin Nation, the "working class" of the white racist movement that advocates violence to achieve its goals. Hammerskins are particularly fond of "white power" music.

Hate groups are also fond of using numbers and letters in symbolic ways. For example, the number 4/20 is a celebration of Adolf Hitler's birth, and 88 is used by neo-Nazis as a greeting (the eighth letter in the alphabet is *H,* so 88 means HH, or "Heil, Hitler"). If you see these numbers in opening or closing parts of letters or e-mail notices, watch out. The number 14 represents a racist creed that is fourteen words long: "We must secure the existence of our people and a future for white children." This creed was spawned by a Northwest group called the Order, which has been traced to bank robberies, arson, and even, in at least one case, the murder of a talk-show host. The number 4/19, which most often shows up as a tattoo, is the anniversary of two events that hate groups commemorate: the confrontation between federal agents and the Branch Davidians in Waco, Texas (in 1993), and the terrible, tragic bombing of a federal building by Timothy McVeigh in 1995.

If you suspect your teenagers may be using these symbols or hanging out with others who do, you can gain more information about their meaning by going to the Anti-Defamation League Web site: <www.adl.org>.

If your teenagers have fallen into the clutches of one of these groups, you need to seek professional help *immediately*. The longer young people stay in such groups, the more harm will be done, and you'll want to enlist the counsel of a trained person to help your children make a clean break. Joining one of these groups shows that something is already wrong with your children's sense of purpose, self-esteem, and social responsibility.

Substance Abuse

Some years ago I worked with a young high school senior who had gone to a party at the local university while visiting a girlfriend. Of course she had a great need to be just like everybody else, so she walked around with a drink in her hand, sipping it whenever someone was looking her way. Unfamiliar with the effects of alcohol, this girl guzzled a little too much too quickly and passed out at the party. Some young men, who were obviously concerned for her welfare, thought enough of her to take her to their apartment. There they removed her clothing and, as best as we could determine, about ten young men gang-raped this seventeen-year-old high school student.

When she finally regained full consciousness several hours later, all she had were some faint, frightening memories of what had taken place. The truth was too ugly to believe, but the soreness below her waist was too real to be ignored. What a devastating memory this young woman has to face.

Alcohol's Ache

Frighteningly at least 3 million American teens abuse alcohol on a regular basis.[11] A survey by the Harvard School of Public

Health found that 44 percent of college students are binge drinkers, and nearly 74 percent said they binged in high school, leading Enoch Gordis, the director of the National Institute on Alcohol Abuse and Alcoholism, to say, "We have a massive alcohol problem among youth."[12] When the Centers for Disease Control surveyed a group of ninth graders, one out of four admitted to binge drinking in the prior month.[13]

Unfortunately this "early experimentation" can have lifelong consequences. Claire Costales, author of *Staying Dry*, became an alcoholic at seventeen. She began drinking at home by sneaking drinks at parties in her own home or at parties in friends' homes, which she attended with her family. Costales says that "if booze hadn't been presented to me as acceptable, helpful and glamorous, chances are I would not have chosen a career in alcoholism."[14]

This tells me that the burden of informing–modeling as well as teaching–our children about this great threat to their happiness, their health, and their very lives is on us, their parents. Remember that children and adolescents copy what is modeled for them, and the earliest modeling they have is in the home. If very young children see one or both parents socializing over liquor, offering it to their guests, they will of course assume that's the proper way to act.

At the same time, however, that you are trying to teach your children liquor is not good for them, they have to wait until they are twenty-one to drink. What does this do? It makes them want it all the more, that much sooner. Alcohol becomes a symbol of "growing up," taking illegal and premature possession of adulthood in a very dangerous way. When adolescents want to impress their peers and act grown up, where do they turn?

That's right: the bottle.

This dangerous cocktail is all the more potent because it's unlikely that adolescents have been prepared in their home for the dynamite effect of alcohol, so the first time they drink at a party could be their last. Read the papers every September: It seems that somewhere around this country, another college student dies of alcohol poisoning at a campus party.

Begin talking about the danger of alcohol to your children when they are very young. A friend of mine goes out of his way to do this. One time he took his son to a sports restaurant to watch a football game. One patron got drunk and started acting so obnoxious that another patron stood up and challenged him to go outside to fight. My friend's son's eyes were wide open.

"Why is he acting like that, Dad?" he asked.

"See that pitcher of beer he's been drinking?" my friend answered.

"Yeah."

"That's what happens when you drink too much. It makes you lose control and do stupid things. Do you ever want to look like that?"

"No way."

"Then stay away from alcohol. That guy's likely to wake up tomorrow with a couple of black eyes, and he may not even remember how it happened!"

This same friend looks for stories of teens who were hurt or even killed due to alcohol and regularly points out the stories to his children. "I want you kids to see this," he says. "If you drink too much, it can literally kill you. If you drink too much and drive, you can kill someone else."

When my kids were young, whenever we came up to a traffic accident, I said, "Probably drugs or alcohol, one or the other."

It got to the point that my kids would beat me to it: "So, Dad," they would say, "think it was drugs or alcohol?"

"Probably."

Parents who want to train their children properly need to become familiar with new studies showing severe consequences for underage drinking. Apart from the obvious—drunk driving, becoming an alcoholic, losing control, and being taken advantage of at a party—researchers are now discovering alarming long-term effects from alcohol abuse.

Kathleen Fackelmann, a reporter for *USA Today*, warns that "preliminary studies indicate that heavy, regular drinking can damage the developing brains of teens and young adults and perhaps destroy brain cells involved in learning and memory." Fackelmann also reports that Dr. Duncan Clark, a researcher at the University of Pittsburgh Medical Center, warns that "the implications" of adolescent use of alcohol "are quite serious," including a loss of memory and a *permanently* affected brain. While this area of study is still somewhat controversial, many researchers now believe that there is a substantial link between alcohol abuse and permanent brain damage.[15]

Of particular concern to parents of daughters is the fact that females can be even more affected than males. It's not a coincidence that my client who passed out was a woman. Due to their physical makeup, males are better able to maintain a constant level of tolerance to alcohol. Because of this, it's easier for a male to gauge how much is too much and when he has gone too far.

The same is not true for women. The blood-alcohol level that an individual woman can tolerate varies greatly, possibly in relation to her menstrual cycle and/or the use of contraceptives. Physiologically it is quite dangerous for adolescent girls to have anything to do with alcohol.

Although I believe it is important for parents to respect their children's privacy, this is one area where we are obliged to be very observant and attentive to avoid any life-threatening situations. Look for these red flags:

- Unexcused absence from school
- Defensive attitude when questioned about alcohol
- Behavioral changes: extreme moodiness, boredom, or exhaustion

- Bottles stashed in the garbage
- An unusual interest in using breath mints and mouthwash

To be safe, you need to know where your adolescents are going and with whom they are going to spend time. From time to time, it's entirely appropriate to check up on them, just to make sure they're being honest. Never allow an adolescent party to take place at your house when you are not present. And make sure your kids know that if they have had too much to drink or if the person who drove them somewhere starts to drink, they can call you and you'll pick them up, without recriminations.

If your teenagers should ever stumble through the door, obviously drunk, take care of their immediate needs, and then get them to bed. The next day, while they still have a pounding head from the night before, be direct and straightforward with them about what happened. Don't waste your ammunition on children in a drunken stupor, however; they won't remember it anyway.

Pothead Personality

Another favorite substance for adolescents to abuse is marijuana, or pot. According to a report by the Harvard School of Public Health, marijuana use among U.S. college students has gone up over the past decade, with 15.7 percent of students now using this drug.[16] Rates have stabilized somewhat, but even one in six college students using pot is still too many.

One of my former clients got sucked into this culture. I'll let him tell his story in his own words:

I started getting high on drugs when I was a freshman in high school. I guess if you were to ask me why I started getting high, I would say it was probably because everybody was doing it, it was the thing to do, and you weren't cool if you weren't doing it. Before I let peer pressure take over, I used to enjoy telling people that I didn't use drugs, drink alcohol, or smoke cigarettes. I can still say truthfully that I've never smoked a whole cigarette, but with dope, you weren't cool if you didn't participate.

I have to admit the first couple of times I tried pot, I didn't get too much out of it, but I kept on doing it and kept on doing it until it got to be where it was a fun thing to do. I'd go to parties, and at first I'd really laugh a lot and it was just a good time. My friends and I would get giggly and all that stuff. The first couple of months it was a lot of fun; it was a cool thing to do. Instead of going to class we'd go out and catch a "buzz." When we came back, everybody saw we had red eyes and thought we were cool. So it was really neat to walk into class and let everybody know we were high.

It wasn't until a couple of years later that I really started having bad feelings about marijuana. I wasn't smart enough to see what it was doing to me, but I could sure see what it was doing to my friends. It seemed that a lot of procrastination was happening in their lives. We'd get high in the morning and just kind of waste the day, just breeze through the whole day, not really accomplish anything, just sit there and watch TV or do nothing. Inside I didn't feel good about just sitting around all day and not doing anything, but that was pretty common with marijuana.

My client found out what many scientists and physicians have now proved: marijuana creates a particular personality in its users. In some people the effects do not show up for several years; in others the personality impairment is almost immediate. These distinct traits are called pot-personality symptoms: impaired short-term memory, emotional flatness, the dropout syndrome (out of sports, school, family, work), diminished will-power, lessened concentration, short attention span, difficulty dealing with abstract or complex problems, low levels of tolerance for frustration, increased confusion in thinking, impaired judgment, and greater hostility toward authority.[17]

What can we do to help our teens avoid this trap? I don't want to sound like a broken record, but virtually everything I've said up to this point needs only to be reinforced. Some years ago I read a research article that confirmed what I have long believed to be true. Cynthia Tudor, David Petersen, and Kirk Elifson demonstrate that the closer adolescents are to their parents, the less likely it is that they will use drugs. The more independent the adolescents are from their parents, the greater the likelihood that they will use drugs.[18]

If you're not taking the time to talk to your children about drugs, start today. Drugs are as accessible to children and adolescents today as Hershey bars were available to us. Talk to your kids about drugs and about the values you want them to have. If you come from a particular faith background, use Scripture to talk about why we shouldn't defile our body (see, for example, 1 Corinthians 6:19-20 and 2 Corinthians 6:14–7:1).

If, in spite of building a close relationship with my children, I came across evidence that they were using drugs, I would be very direct. It's good psychological advice to force a "blow out" rather than watch your children's lives be gradually drained away by drugs. I wouldn't ask my children if they were using drugs because druggies, frankly (next to politicians), are the world's biggest liars. Instead I would say, "I know you're using drugs, and I'm very upset and very disappointed at what you're doing."

The next thing I would do is make sure to keep my money under lock and key. Money is the pipeline that keeps drugs flowing, and often drug users do not have jobs. I would regularly count the money in my pocket and not leave my money in a place where it could be stolen.

Frankly I would do just about anything to get my children out of this situation because cocaine and other drugs destroy people's lives. I don't mind scaring you if it will give you the motivation you need to get involved. A number of years ago I had to make one of the most difficult phone calls of my life. A young man enrolled in a university had some beers and then popped some barbiturates, failing to pay any attention to the professionals who warn that the combination of drugs and alcohol can be fatal. Early in the morning his roommate returned from his night on the town and noticed something very peculiar about this young man—his neck was blue.

In fact, he was dead. I would be willing to bet that his parents never took the time to talk with their son about the deadly nature of drugs.

Perhaps those parents didn't know where to begin or didn't have the necessary information. There's no excuse for that today. Every community has all kinds of information about drug use, and any number of Web sites provide up-to-date educational materials. The reality of life today is that drugs are easily available. It is all but certain that your kids will have to make a choice whether or not they will use drugs. The question is not whether the opportunity will present itself but how your children will respond when it does.

Are your adolescents prepared?

Where Do I Draw the Line?

A frequently asked question goes something like this: "When is enough enough? That is, when should I finally kick a troublesome kid out of the house?"

Most often troublesome kids will tell you themselves when it's time for them to go. If a disruptive eighteen-year-old son said to me, "I can do whatever I want to do; you have no authority over me," I would calmly say, "You're absolutely right, and now might be a good time for you to move out on your own. In this home we live in concert with each other and have respect for each other. If you are insistent on coming home at four o'clock in the morning and smoking in your room, then it's time for you to get your own place."

Kids need to understand that parents have some rights too. While we love our children and often make sacrifices on their behalf, we needn't become prisoners to their hostility and poor choices. I wouldn't, for instance, put up with a son who invited his drug-dealing friends into my home. That's flat-out dangerous, with possible illegal activity going on.

Another factor to consider is whether you have younger kids. When teenagers' lifestyles become so disruptive that they are influencing my younger kids, well, let me just say they won't be smoking it up in my house! At a certain age, staying in my home becomes a privilege, not a right, and if children abuse that privilege, they lose the opportunity as well.

Remember:

- Eating disorders are a cry for help, requiring immediate professional intervention.
- Suicide attempts peak in midadolescence, so take depression seriously.
- Running away isn't uncommon among adolescents; in order to know how to respond, you need to know your children and your neighborhood.
- Hate groups step in when families fail to create a sense of belonging.
- Substance abuse is rampant among today's youth; your children will be presented with an opportunity to abuse alcohol and drugs, so they need to be prepared.
- Children and adolescents copy what is modeled for them, and the earliest modeling they have is in the home.

Epilogue

A Teenager's
Ten Commandments
to Parents

IF THE ROAD GETS rocky, allow me to encourage you with words I've already stated but want to reiterate: Adolescence truly isn't terminal. Even jerks can come out of these trying times and do okay.

I know—I was a jerk myself. You've heard about some of my antics already, but perhaps you didn't realize how hopeless my life looked when I was eighteen years old. My guidance counselor was brutally honest: "Leman," he told me, "with your grades, I couldn't get you into reform school." My mother prayed all through my high school years for just one C on my report card as a sign from God that there really was gray matter between my ears.

Hope springs eternal, so my parents and I sent off an application to North Park College, a Christian school that we thought might have mercy. Here are the two letters we got back:

FOSTER AND KEDZIE AVENUES • CHICAGO 25, ILLINOIS

NORTH PARK COLLEGE *and Theological Seminary*

ACADEMY • COLLEGE • SEMINARY

FOUNDED 1891

July 3, 1961

Mr. Kevin Leman
204 Ridgewood Drive
Snyder 26, New York

Dear Mr. Leman:

Earlier I deferred action on your application for admission to North
Park College pending an evaluation of your seventh semester of high
school studies. In studying the transcript for the semester just
completed I find, to my regret, that you have not shown sufficient
strength to warrant an acceptance at this time. Therefore, I must
decline your application.

You may desire to use the services of the College Admissions Center in
any further inquiries you may wish to make. This activity is directed
by the Association of College Admissions Counselors. The Center should
be addressed at the North Shore Hotel, Chicago Avenue at Davis Street,
Evanston, Illinois.

Be sure of my personal unhappiness in the decision I must make, and
also of my best wishes for you.

Sincerely yours,

Oscar E. Olson
Director of Admissions and Records

OEO:ve

In Thy Light shall we see Light

FOSTER AND KEDZIE AVENUES • CHICAGO 25, ILLINOIS

FOUNDED 1891

NORTH PARK COLLEGE *and Theological Seminary*

ACADEMY • COLLEGE • SEMINARY

July 3, 1961

Mr. and Mrs. John Leman
204 Ridgewood
Snyder 26, N.Y.

Dear Mr. and Mrs. Leman:

I am writing to you at this time for two reasons: to explain our admissions policy and to indicate my intended action on your son's application.

Our admissions policy is built on two major premises and involve judgment of ourselves as well as the student. We must satisfy ourselves that we can meet the needs of the student. We must also satisfy ourselves that the student can meet our standards.

Included in our responsibility for satisfying the student's needs is the curriculum choice and also, sometimes, special attention or remedial studies.

In the area of standards we have found that the high school record is the best single predictor of success in college. When we add standardized test evidence we get an even stronger prediction.

Presently we are granting admission to students who rank in the upper one-half of their high school classes. Students in the lower half whose records show strong improvement in their junior year and whose test data are encouraging will be acted upon after the final semester's grades are received.

Most regrettably, Kevin's record does not support admission. Rather, therefore, than grant him a probationary semester in which, our studies show, he would likely be unsuccessful, I must decline his application. However, if he should begin his college program in some other school and earn a C average in his first 15 semester hours I would be glad to review his application.

I cannot close this letter without thanking you for the confidence in North Park that Kevin's application demonstrates. I believe that we will continue to enjoy your support and good will. A message to Kevin informing him of my decision will follow this letter.

Sincerely yours,

Oscar E. Olson
Director of Admissions and Records
In Thy Light shall we see Light
OEO:ve

You know what's so amazing? These letters had been lost for decades; my assistant came across them recently in an old file, and when she called to tell me the good news, I stopped her and said I bet I could recite them from memory. Debbie was shocked as, over the phone, I recited from memory a letter that was over forty years old. The rejection was so embedded in my mind that even today it makes its mark.

Don't misunderstand me. I'm in no way faulting Oscar Olson, who wrote those letters. If I had had Oscar's job, I would have slam-dunked my application in the rejection bin too. In fact, I probably would have called a technical foul on me for having the audacity to even send in the application!

But God does move in mysterious ways. Nine days before the semester started, Oscar Olson relented and allowed me to enter North Park on probation with a light, twelve-unit load. (I sent him a Scripture verse about forgiveness, and I think that really helped!) I'm indebted to North Park for giving me the chance that no one else would. I think so much of them that Sande and I later sent our second-born daughter, Krissy, to school there.

Back then few people thought I was going to do anything or go anywhere—except my parents. Through it all, I knew my mom and dad loved me and cared for me. That makes a tremendous difference in a kid's life—even a scatterbrained kid's life.

Parents, there is hope. Don't give up. Adolescence can be a rocky time, but it has an end. If you love your children and follow the principles we've discussed in this book, I believe, in time, your children will come around.

Let's part with some final advice that will help you bring them there. These short words of mine, written almost two decades ago, have been copied by many leaders and teachers, and I'm pleased to include them here:

A Teenager's Ten Commandments to Parents

1. Please don't give me everything I say I want. Saying no shows me you care. I appreciate guidelines.

2. Don't treat me as if I were a little kid. Even though you know what's "right," I need to discover some things for myself.

3. Respect my need for privacy. Often I need to be alone to sort things out and daydream.

4. Never say, "In my day . . ." That's an immediate turn off. Besides, the pressures and responsibilities of my world are more complicated than they were when you were my age.

5. I don't pick your friends or clothes; please don't criticize mine. We can disagree and still respect each other's choices.

6. Refrain from always rescuing me; I learn most from my mistakes. Hold me accountable for the decisions I make in life; it's the only way I'll learn to be responsible.

7. Be brave enough to share your disappointments, thoughts, and feelings with me. By the way, I'm never too old to be told I'm loved.

8. Don't talk in volumes. I've had years of good instruction; now trust me with the wisdom you have shared.

9. I respect you when you ask me for forgiveness for a thoughtless deed or word on your part. It proves that neither of us is perfect.

10. Set a good example for me as God intended you to do. I pay more attention to your actions than your words.

Notes

Chapter 1: What Planet Am I On?

1. Gary Levin, "Graduating Class an Optimistic Bunch," *USA Today*, 22 June 2000, sec. D, p. 6.
2. Marsha Rosenbaum, "Just Say No—or Just Know?" *USA Today*, 10 July 2000, sec. A, p. 17.
3. Dan Vergano, "Teens May Be Hooked within First Days of Smoking," *USA Today*, 12 September 2000, sec. D, p. 1.
4. Stephanie Armour, "Baby-Faced Retirees Cash Out, Carry On," *USA Today*, 5 October 2000, sec. D, p. 2.
5. SADD/Liberty Mutual, "Teens Today" report, *USA Today*, 13 September 2000, sec. D, p. 6.
6. Sheila Rayam, "Girls Precocious but Unprepared," *USA Today*, 13 September 2000, sec. D, p. 8.
7. Amy Larocca, "How Little Marshall Mathers Became a Badass," *George* (September 2000): 76.
8. Ibid.
9. Ibid., 77.
10. See the Web site at <www.arod.com>.

Chapter 2: Twenty Rules for Surviving Your Kids' Adolescence

1. Nancy Collins, "The Unsinkable Spirit of Michael J. Fox," *George* (October 2000): 122.

Chapter 3: Percolating Peer Pressure

1. Michael W. Smith, *This Is Your Time* (Nashville: Nelson, 2000), 70–71.
2. Ibid., 118.

Chapter 4: Planet Peer Pressure

1. Tamara Henry, "Survey Takes Measure of Widespread Hazing," *USA Today*, 29 August 2000, sec. D, p. 1.
2. Ibid.
3. "Boys and Girls Differ on Definition of Cool," *USA Today*, 14 August 2000, sec. D, p. 6.

Chapter 5: The Fairy-Tale Lifestyle

1. David Blankenhorn, "Dads, Daughters Forge Key Bonds," *USA Today*, 8 May 2000, sec. A, p. 19.

2. Department of Health and Human Services, Morehouse Report, National Center for Children in Poverty, U.S. Bureau of the Census, cited in "What Father Involvement Means," *USA Today*, 30 May 2000, sec. A, p. 10.

3. Anita Manning, "Absent Dads Scar Millions . . . ," *USA Today*, 7 June 2000, sec. D, p. 7.

4. Jonetta Barras, quoted in Manning, "Absent Dads Scar Millions . . . ," sec. D, p. 7.

5. Blankenhorn, "Dads, Daughters Forge Key Bonds."

6. Ibid.

7. Ibid.

8. Marvin Olasky, "Divorce Undermines Joy, Hope at Graduation Time," *USA Today*, 18 May 1998, sec. A, p. 19.

Chapter 6: The Great Transfer

1. Stephanie Mansfield, "Sarah's Sexy Success," *USA Weekend* (May 26–28, 2000): 7.

2. "Kids Roam Free," *Bellingham (Wash.) Herald*, 5 October 2000, sec. C, p. 1.

3. David Popenoe and Barbara Dafoe Whitehead, "Sex without Strings, Relationships without Rings," The National Marriage Project, Rutgers University (2000); <www.marriage.Rutgers.edu>.

4. Sheila Rayam, "Most Teens Admit Cheating on Tests, Lying to Parents," *USA Today*, 16 October 2000, sec. D, p. 8.

5. Lynn Okagaki, Kimberly Hammound, and Laura Seamon, "Socialization of Religious Beliefs," *Journal of Applied Developmental Psychology* 20, no. 2 (2000): 273–294.

6. Ibid., 283.

7. Ibid., 290–291.

8. Kevin Leman, *What a Difference a Daddy Makes* (Nashville: Nelson, 2000), 126–127.

Chapter 7: Everyday Hassles

1. "School Fashion Fuss," *USA Today*, 25 September 2000, sec. D, p. 1.

2. "Mail Call," *GQ* (August 1999): 32.

3. Dr. Bruce Narramore, "Teenage Negativism: How Much Is Normal?" *Psychology for Living* (September-October 2000): 9.

4. Ibid.

5. Ibid., 22.

Chapter 8: Risky Business

1. This story is based on Jay Carty's verbal account, which he also mentions in his book *Counter Attack* (Santa Barbara: Yes! Ministries, 1988), 137–138.

Chapter 9: Toxic Parents

1. Ann Landers, "Teen Works Hard but Dad Still Yells," *Orlando Sentinel,* 20 October 2000, sec. E, p. 3.
2. Cited in Marilyn Elias, "Teens Take Brunt of Parents' Verbal Abuse," *USA Today,* 15 August 2000, sec. D, p. 7.
3. Ibid.
4. Patrick Welsh, "Posting Kids' Grades on the Net Just Asks for Trouble," *USA Today,* 5 June 2000, sec. A, p. 17.
5. Ibid.
6. Ibid.
7. If you want help with this, see my book *When Your Best Isn't Good Enough* (Grand Rapids: Revell, 1997).
8. These examples as well as the rest of the illustrations in this section are taken from William Nack and Lester Munson, "Out of Control," *Sports Illustrated* (July 24, 2000): 88–89.
9. David Popenoe and Barbara Dafoe Whitehead, "Sex without Strings, Relationships without Rings," The National Marriage Project, Rutgers University (2000); <www.marriage.Rutgers.edu>.
10. Ibid., 21–22.
11. Jeffrey Zaslow, "Julian Lennon on His Dad," *USA Weekend* (May 28–30, 1999): 22.

Chapter 10: Dr. Leman, You Can't Be Serious!

1. Ruth La Ferla, "Teens Today Go for Gucci," New York Times News Service, *Bellingham (Wash.) Herald,* 14 September 2000, sec. C, p. 1.
2. Patrick Welsh, "Oh, Those Prom Bills . . . ," *USA Today,* 21 June 1999, sec. A, p. 23.
3. Ibid.
4. Ibid.
5. Ibid.

Chapter 12: Sex and the Adolescent

1. Centers for Disease Control, "Trends in Sexual Risk Behaviors among High School Students–United States, 1991–1997," *Morbidity and Mortality Weekly Report* (Sept. 18, 1998): 749–752.
2. The Alan Guttmacher Institute, "Issues in Brief: Teenage Pregnancy and the Welfare Reform Debate," 1998; <www.agi-usa.org/pubs/ib5.html>.
3. The Alan Guttmacher Institute, as cited in Karen S. Peterson, "Younger Kids Trying It Now . . . ," *USA Today,* 16 November 1999, sec. D, p. 1.
4. Robert Blum, as cited in Peterson, "Younger Kids."

5. Ibid., sec. D, p. 2.
6. The Alan Guttmacher Institute, "Facts in Brief: Teen Sex and Pregnancy," September 1999; <www.agi-usa.org/pubs/fb_teen_sex.html>.
7. Marilyn Elias, "Chats with Parents Pass Sex Attitudes to Teens," *USA Today,* 7 August 2000, sec. D, p. 6.
8. Ibid.
9. Kelly Ettenborough, *Arizona Republic,* carried in *Bellingham (Wash.) Herald,* 7 December 2000, sec. C, p. 6.

Chapter 13: The Seamy Side of Sex

1. Archibald Hart, *The Sexual Man* (Dallas: Word, 1994), 46.
2. National Center for Health Statistics News Release, "New CDC Birth Report Shows Teen Birth Rates Continue to Drop," August 8, 2000; <www.cdc.gov/nchs/releases/00news/newbirth.htm>.
3. The Alan Guttmacher Institute, "Facts in Brief: Teen Sex and Pregnancy," September 1999; <www.agi-usa.org/pubs/fb_teen_sex.html>.
4. National Center for Health Statistics, "Preventing Teenage Pregnancy," Feb. 29, 2000; <www.cdc.gov/nchs/about/major/natality/teenpreg.htm>.
5. Centers for Disease Control, "Trends in Sexual Risk Behaviors among High School Students–United States, 1991–1997," *Morbidity and Mortality Weekly Report* (September 18, 1998): 747–752.
6. This chart, used by crisis pregnancy centers, is based on this formula: If N is the number of sexual partners, then the number of exposures for each of those partners is computed as [(2 to the Nth power) - 1]. Why the subtraction of 1? Because the person's exposure to himself or herself is not the problem!
7. Guttmacher Institute, "Teen Sex."
8. Karen Thomas, "Kids Run a 20% Risk of 'Cybersex' Advances," *USA Today,* 8 June 2000, sec. A, p. 1.
9. Visit the Web site at <netaddiction.com/index.html>.
10. The characteristics listed in this section are from Kimberly Young, author of *Caught in the Net: How to Recognize the Signs of Internet Addiction* (New York: John Wiley and Sons, 1998), quoted in Jane Brody, "Cybersex Joins Ranks of Addiction," *Bellingham (Wash.) Herald,* 17 May 2000, sec. C, p. 3.
11. These names are being used only as generic examples; neither is, to my knowledge, an actual company.
12. Real Families Club offers free Internet software to keep pornography off your computer. Visit the Web site at <www.realfamilies.com>, or call toll free 1-877-4RealUs. When you sign up, we'll send you a copy of my best-selling book, *Sex Begins in the Kitchen,* along with some free magazine subscriptions.

13. U.S. Bureau of the Census, *Marital Status and Living Arrangements* (March 1998); <www.census.gov>.

14. Larry Bumpass and Hsien-Hen Lu, "Trends in Cohabitation and Implication for Children's Family Context" (Madison, Wisc.: Center for Demography, University of Wisconsin, 1998), cited in Andrew R. Baker, "Cohabitation Fails as a Test for Marriage," *Homiletic and Pastoral Review* (May 2000).

15. Catherine Cohan, quoted in Karen Peterson, "Cohabiters May Miscommunicate," *USA Today*, 18 July 2000, sec. D, p. 8.

16. David Popenoe and Barbara Dafoe Whitehead, "Sex without Strings, Relationships without Rings," The National Marriage Project, Rutgers University (2000); <www.marriage.Rutgers.edu>.

Chapter 14: Troubled Teens

1. Vicki Harvey, "Understanding Eating Disorders," *Psychology for Living* (September-October 2000): 7.

2. Ibid., 8.

3. Remuda Ranch has an outstanding program for eating disorders. Contact them at Remuda Ranch, One E. Apache Street, Wickenburg, Arizona 85390; (520) 684-3913, (800) 445-1900; <www.remuda_ranch.com>.

4. Harvey, "Understanding Eating Disorders," 8.

5. Ibid.

6. David Murphy, "Suicidal Thoughts Aren't Normal . . . ," *Bellingham (Wash.) Herald*, 11 September 1999, sec. C, p. 7.

7. Ibid.

8. David Satcher, *Mental Health: A Report of the Surgeon General* (Washington, D.C.: U.S. Government, 1999).

9. Ibid.

10. Ibid.

11. Kathleen Fackelmann, "Teen Drinking, Thinking Don't Mix," *USA Today*, 18 October 2000, sec. D, p. 1.

12. Ibid.

13. Kathleen Fackelmann, "Schools Urged to Serve the Facts about Booze," *USA Today*, 18 October 2000, sec. D, p. 8.

14. Claire Costales, *Staying Dry* (Ventura, Calif.: Regal Books, 1980), 30.

15. Duncan Clark, quoted in Fackelmann, "Teen Drinking."

16. Michelle Healy, "More College Students Use Marijuana," *USA Today*, 31 October 2000, sec. D, p. 9.

17. Peggy Mann, "Marijuana Alert III: The Devastation of Personality," *Reader's Digest* (December 1981): 81.

18. Cynthia Tudor, David Petersen, and Kirk Elifson, "An Examination of the Relationship between Peer and Parental Influences and Adolescent Drug Use," *Adolescence* (winter 1980): 795.

About the Author

Dr. Kevin Leman, internationally known psychologist, author, and speaker, has taught and entertained audiences worldwide with his wit and commonsense psychology. Leman is the founder and president of Couples of Promise, an organization designed and committed to helping couples remain happily married.

In addition to cohosting the television program *realFAMILIES,* Leman is a regular guest on national radio and television talk shows, including *Focus on the Family, The View,* the *Today* show, *The Oprah Winfrey Show, Live with Regis Philbin, CNN, The 700 Club,* and *Life Today* with James Robison. He has also served as a consulting family psychologist for ABC's *Good Morning America.*

Dr. Leman has written twenty-three books about marriage and family issues, including *The New Birth Order Book, Sex Begins in the Kitchen, When Your Best Is Not Good Enough, Making Children Mind without Losing Yours, Women Who Try Too Hard, Becoming a Couple of Promise, What a Difference a Daddy Makes, Making Sense of the Men in Your Life,* and *The Birth Order Connection.*

Dr. Leman attended North Park College and received his bachelor's degree in psychology from the University of Arizona, where he later earned his master's degree and doctorate. He and his wife, Sande, live in Tucson, Arizona, and have four daughters and one son.

For additional information about video and audio resources, or about speaking-engagement information for businesses, churches, and civic organizations, please contact:

Dr. Kevin Leman
P.O. Box 35370
Tucson, Arizona 85740
Phone: (520) 797-3830
Fax: (520) 797-3809

Toll-free number for realFAMILIES Club: (877) 4REALUS
Web site: realfamilies.com